THE DEVIL'S DICTIONARY

THE

The Devil's Dictionary

AMBROSE BIERCE

Illustrated by

RALPH STEADMAN

Introduction by Angus Calder

BLOOMSBURY

Introduction copyright © 2003 by Angus Calder

Illustrations and display face (Cheltenham Spa bold)
copyright © 2003 by Ralph Steadman

Published by Bloomsbury, New York and London
Distributed to the trade by Holtzbrinck Publishers

All papers used by Bloomsbury are natural, recyclable products made from
wood grown in sustainable, well-managed forests. The manufacturing processes
conform to the environmental regulations of the country of origin.

Library of Congress Cataloging-in-Publication Data

Bierce, Ambrose, 1842-1914?
    The Devil's dictionary / Ambrose Bierce; illustrated by Ralph
Steadman; Introduction by Angus Calder.— 1st U.S. ed.
        p. cm.
    Abridged edition.
    ISBN 1-58234-380-2
    1. English language—Dictionaries—Humor. 2. English language—
Semantics—Humor 3. Vocabulary—Humor. I. Steadman, Ralph
II. Title.

PS1097.D4 2004
423'.02'07--dc22

2003060521

First U.S. Edition 2003

1 3 5 7 9 10 8 6 4 2

Typeset in Bembo by Palimpsest Book Production Limited,
Polmont, Stirlingshire, Scotland
Printed in Great Britain by
Butler and Tanner Ltd, Frome and London

CONTENTS

INTRODUCTION
Angus Calder

Ambrose Bierce (1842-1913?) despised realism. In his *Devil's Dictionary* he defines it as 'The art of depicting nature as it is seen by toads . . . or a story written by a measuring worm.' Assuming that his own life was a fiction, who would credit as 'realistic' either its beginning or end – the bizarre circumstance of his naming, 'Ambrose Gwynett,' and the extraordinary fact that one of America's most celebrated literary men and public figures could disappear totally without trace on an actual or fabricated excursion into Mexico to view the battles of its revolution?

Rather more mundanely, there is a staring contradiction between the personality projected in his journalistic writings – that of a cynical misanthrope and intractable misogynist, despairing of all politicians and their isms, venomously antipathetic to all religious belief and to clerics of every known or conceivable creed, and scathing in his invective against writers, famous and obscure, whom he considered bad – and the person exposed by attentive biographers. The atrabilious Bierce persona of the *Dictionary* was the mask of a much hurt man.

Though he quarrelled with many friends sooner or later, he always had ample to choose from. Perhaps because they thought they knew that his contempt for females was a pose, numerous women were amongst the young writers

vii

who flocked for advice to the Dr. Johnson of San Francisco, the literary arbiter of West Coast America, and to whom he was unflaggingly kind and supportive. 'Bitter Bierce', 'The Wickedest Man in San Francisco,' somehow survived, with a rich sunset glow of reputation, a long journalistic career in which he raked with wit and sarcasm which resounded across America and then over the Atlantic, fellow writers as famous as Henry James and Stephen Crane, all Freemasons, exorbitantly wealthy capitalists, several Presidents – and also obscure preachers, grafting local officials and feeble poetasters.

We cannot recapture whatever charm it was in Bierce made contemporaries tolerate, relish and even love the great 'curmudgeon.' Suffice it to point out, as brief accounts of his life tend not to, that he was an extraordinarily handsome man. He was tall and stood very straight, fit-seeming, though he had chronic asthma. His fair hair flourished, his moustache was magnificent. His eyes were clear blue and his complexion fresh and rosy despite his habitual excesses with strong drink. He dressed very stylishly indeed and was obsessively committed to personal hygiene, perhaps because he had spent the formative years of his life in the stench and filth of one of the nastiest conflicts in human history.

He was born on 24 June 1842, in Meigs County, Ohio. He was the tenth child of Laura and Marcus '*Aurelius*' Bierce. Father, an indigent farmer and devout Congregationalist puritan, descended, like Mother, from seventeenth-century settlers in New England, decided that each child's name should begin with A – Abigail, Amelia, Ann, Addison, Aurelius, Augustus, Almeda, Andrew, Albert – then Ambrose. But how had Marcus come by the melodramatic play by the English writer Jerrold – *Ambrose Gwynett; or A Seaside Story* (1828), which gave him a G to go with the infant's A?

Further As followed – Arthur who died in 1846 aged nine months, then twin girls, Adelia and Aurelia, both dead within two years. Understanding of Ambrose surely has to begin with the fact that as his own understanding dawned, his mother was preoccupied firstly with caring for infants, secondly with mourning successive losses. Woman did not give Boy the love he needed. Rejecting Parents and Family, Ambrose took to books. Marcus was said to have the largest library in Kosciusko County, Indiana, where the family moved in 1846. Here Boy browsed.

Ambrose was a loner, unhappy both at home and school. When he turned fifteen, he quit the homestead for good, at first working as a printer's 'devil' on the Abolitionist newspaper recently founded in the nearby town of Warsaw. Thence he gravitated to Akron, Ohio, where Marcus's very different younger brother Lucius was the most prominent local citizen – lawyer, published author, four times mayor, and military legend. In 1838, Canada had seethed with rebellion against British rule. 'General' Bierce had led a force of 500 volunteers across Lake Erie to stir things up. Now he was a fierce Abolitionist, who provided arms and ammunition for John Brown when the latter set off on his bloody sortie into the proslavery South.

Lucius decided that Ambrose should be a soldier. He sent him, aged seventeen, to the celebrated Kentucky Military Institute. Ambrose dropped out after only one year, but acquired a military bearing and skills in design and cartography which quite soon became very useful indeed. For nine months, Ambrose drifted through menial jobs in Warsaw. Then in the spring of 1861, Civil War erupted. Bierce was one of the first to enlist in Lincoln's army.

With the Ninth Indiana Volunteer Infantry Regiment, Bierce entered diurnal trauma. Twenty thousand British soldiers had died in the recent Crimean War, only 3,000 directly in combat. In the appalling Battle of Shiloh in April 1862, in which Bierce took part, there were 23,741 casualties. All his service was in the South. For a son of the flat Midwest, the mountainous terrain was breathtaking. Its beauty, with agonizing irony, was backdrop to scenes of futile heroism, nightmare butchery. Bierce saw hogs feeding on the corpses of dead soldiers, brains oozing out of shattered skulls. In a sense he had a 'good war'. His extreme bravery attracted attention early on, when he rescued a wounded comrade under Confederate fire. His Kentucky Institute year further marked him for promotion. In February 1862, already a sergeant, he was reassigned to General William B. Hazen's brigade in Buell's Army of the Ohio, and named topographical officer, surveying terrain. In a year, he rose to first lieutenant. By November 1864 he was brevet captain. Close to Staff, he observed with disgust the behavior of generals, some silly, others callous. His hero was Hazen, who suffered no folly gladly, whether in infantrymen or senior commanders.

The future author of *The Devil's Dictionary* had inherited from his Puritan forebears a very strict conscience. Thus he was appalled by what he saw as a Federal treasury agent in Selma, Alabama after his demobilization. Carpetbaggers had moved in to loot the South. Bierce's job was to find and impound cotton deemed to belong to the US government. This was a commodity in immense demand, as important in its way as oil today. Fellow agents were in cahoots with conscienceless businessmen and outright pirates and smugglers. Bierce's stubborn probity put his life at risk. By now he had seen through the bombastic idealism of Uncle Lucius. What had the war really been about? From the careerism of soldiers to the cupidity of public servants, the war and its aftermath had helped provide Bierce, an affronted moralist, with the cynical view of human nature found in *The Devil's Dictionary*

Hazen rescued him with a call to join him in an inspection tour of forts in the newly created Mountain District in the West. Launched in July 1866, this was a risky but exhilarating jaunt, through Indian country where buffalo still roamed. Bierce arrived in San Francisco at the end of the expedition expecting to receive word that he had been commissioned as a captain in the US Army. The letter he now opened offered him the rank of second lieutenant. He was furious and decided to resign. So he found himself jobless in a booming city created within the last two decades by the famous Gold Rush. He would stay there, mostly, for over thirty years.

At first he was employed as a watchman in the US Branch Mint, while he labored on his self education. He read the whole of Edward Gibbon's *Decline and Fall of the Roman Empire*, and this was crucial to the emergence of Bitter Bierce from the chrysalis of a wannabe peacetime soldier. Here Bierce read of a mighty republic fallen into chaos and doomed to erratic Caesarism, of virtuous rulers succeeded by vicious tyrants. Already alienated from his parents' chilly piety and disgusted by the revivalist meetings of rustic evangelists, he would find in Gibbon's ironic explorations of superstition, hypocrisy and corruption in the early Christian Church an intellectual dimension for his intestinal reactions. Not only the views but echoes of the style of the great master pervade Bierce's *Devil's Dictionary*, whenever it ventures into orotund Latinity.

San Francisco was just the place to start as a writer. A population of around one hundred thousand supported towards ninety newspapers and journals of various kinds. Two cardinal pioneers of what had been lacking – a distinctively 'American' literature – were stars in the city's eccentric, self-made firmament: Bret Harte and Mark Twain. Bierce's first publication, in the *Californian*, was a poem. He would write verse for the rest of his career, some of it plangent, more of it satirical, all of it technically sound, and he would always believe that poetry was the highest form of literature. But around this time he decided, with sadness, that he would never be up with the best 'It was the bitterest moment of my life' (O'Connor, 265). He began to publish articles here and there. In the summer of 1868 he joined the staff of the *News Letter*, and by December he was editing that paper. His predecessor, one Watkins, before he left for New York, kindly introduced Bierce to the writings of Swift and Voltaire. From the mad Dean he would have learnt how far savage indignation might proceed in the direction of grimly hilarious bad taste. From the Frenchman he must have imbibed a method of irony, laconic and perky, at a polar extreme from Gibbon's. On the same page of Bierce's *Dictionary*, the somewhat Swift-like suggestion that **Lap** is 'chiefly useful in rural festivities to support plates of cold chicken and the heads of adult males' is followed by the Voltairean **Lawyer** . . . 'One skilled in circumvention of the law.'

The proprietor of the *News Letter*, an Englishman, Frederick Marriott, had made it San Francisco's most profitable advertising organ. He was perfectly happy that Bierce, writing as 'Town Crier,' should increase his circulation by a wholesale onslaught on the city's clergy. Outraged responses poured in. Bierce denounced crimes by Christians against the industrious Chinese community, and commented on murders and suicides. Murder most foul is still a staple circulation-booster. In a time and place where much in the papers was combative and abusive the whole of San Francisco reacted with shock or glee to Town Crier's exceptional, Swiftian, absence of inhibition.

The rising star found a desirable mate in Mollie Day, daughter of a successful miner. Bierce was already attracting attention in London, still the literary capital of English-speakers. Old man Day was happy to send the young couple to England, and in 1872, Bierce sailed eastward-ho.

Other Californian luminaries obeyed the same magnet. Bret Harte would actually settle in England. Mark Twain showed up, as did Joaquin Miller, the self-styled cowboy 'Poet of the Sierras.' But Bierce preferred the tavern company of a group of well-known English fiction writers and journalists, at which W. S. Gilbert, Sullivan's librettist, sometimes appeared. Bierce found publishers for three collections of prose pieces. His pseudonym, 'Dod Grile', an anagram for 'God Riled,' did not become a household name, and Bierce struggled somewhat to support his wife and two infant sons. But he enjoyed England – indeed, became an out-and-out Anglophile – and was not pleased when Mollie, who had retreated, homesick, to San Francisco, announced that she was pregnant with a third child. By October 1875, Bierce was with his family in California, now in economic depression, so that it was many months before he could find a new writing job, contributing a column called 'The Prattler' to the *Argonaut*, 'Town Crier' under a new name.

In 1880 he suddenly skipped away from journalism to go as general manager of a mining company to the Black Hills of Dakota. This was the West at its Wildest and Bierce prudently hired the fastest surviving gun in the region as his company's dedicated heavy, noting him in the payrolls as 'Boone May, murderer.' There was gold in them thar hills, but not where Bierce's company could get it, and through no fault of his own – he was perennially efficient in whatever post he held – the enterprise collapsed within months. But he resumed his 'Prattle' column for yet another San

Francisco journal, *Wasp*, which hired him as editor in January 1881. It was now that he commenced, beginning perversely with P, a series of definitions for his readers as particles of what he called 'The Devil's Dictionary.' It was a popular feature, and eighty-eight installments of fifteen to twenty words each appeared over five years.

The great watershed in Bierce's literary life occurred in 1887. William Randolph Hearst, Harvard-educated son of a filthy-rich self-made Senator, had perceived that the future of the newspaper press lay in shameless 'yellow' sensationalism. He grabbed Bierce to write a column and editorials for his San Francisco *Examiner.* That the man could be guaranteed to be controversial was enough – Hearst did not mind if Bierce uttered opinions contrary to his own. Furthermore, the *Examiner* provided Bierce with an outlet for the Civil War stories which would gain him recognition as a major American creative writer.

The short story was still in its adolescence as a literary genre. What Bierce brought to the form was a combination of careful detail with grotesque and extraordinary incidents 'beyond belief.' He has been seen as a precursor of the 'magical realism' of the later twentieth century. Yet he would have regarded himself as harking back to Walter Scott, the great 'Romancer.' See his *Dictionary*, under **Novel**: '. . . To the romance the novel is what photography is to a painting.' An acute editor of Bierce's stories perceives 'continuity' between those about the Civil War and his 'tall tales' and tales of the supernatural set in civilian life (Quirk, xxiv). But the latter catered for existing public taste. There had been nothing in English like the Civil War stories, which retain their power to shock after all the remarkable writing about war seen since 1914. Even Robert Graves, say, or Vasily Grossman seem to be holding something back from us, in charity, when compared to Bierce's unsparing 'Chickamauga.'

Bierce had been serving with Hazen's brigade in Georgia when the Battle of Chickamauga had erupted in September 1863. It was 'the bloodiest two-day encounter of the entire war,' from which the Northern Army retreated leaving some 16000 dead and wounded behind them (Morris, 56-65). As old soldiers do, Bierce had choked back his most horrific memories, literally unspeakable, for decades. His art at last gave Chickamauga stylized, not 'photographic', shape by seeing its aftermath from the point of view of a deaf-mute little boy.

Tales of Soldiers and Civilians, his first book of fiction, appeared in 1891. Bierce's rush of 'serious' creativity coincided with personal calamity. He was outraged to discover a love letter written to Mollie by a Danish visitor to California. Perhaps, for the vocal decrier of marriage, it was pretext, not just cause, of his breaking from her in 1888, but he would tell their daughter years later that Mollie had been the love of his life. Next year, their son Day, aged seventeen, a budding journalist, killed himself after shooting his best friend over a girl.

Bierce wrote bitterly on. Affable, and generous with pay though Hearst was, Bierce perceived and mistrusted his political agenda. (His populist newspapers were intended to help Hearst become President.) But his employer's cause was his own in 1896 when Hearst sent him to Washington to campaign against Collis P. Huntington.

Bierce loathed Huntington, veteran survivor of a generation of unbridled post-Civil War capitalists. The Lincoln administration had loaned money to his Southern Pacific railroad company. No interest had been paid, and now Huntington had sponsored a bill in Congress proposing a seventy-five year postponement of the debt. For months,

Bierce filed devastating copy to Hearst's San Francisco and New York newspapers. One day, on the steps of the Capitol, Huntington asked Bierce to name his price. "'My price,'" said Bierce, in a quote that would make newspaper headlines across the country, "is seventy-five million dollars. If, when you are ready to pay, I happen to be out of town, you may hand it over to my friend, the Treasurer of the United States'" (Morris, 226). Huntington was duly thwarted in Congress.

In December 1899, Bierce returned to live in Washington, permanently, still hired to write for Hearst. He was sadly on hand when his second son Leigh, also a journalist, died of pneumonia in New York early in 1901. Mollie Bierce died four years later, shortly after filing for divorce at last. Meanwhile, from 1904 Bierce produced for Hearst twenty-four more installments of his dictionary. *The Cynic's Word Book* appeared in 1906 – his publishers, Doubleday, were squeamish as to title. This was a collected set of *Devil's Dictionary* definitions, but only from A to L. The entire alphabet was published in 1911, under the correct title, in Volume 7 of an ill-advised twelve volume *Collected Works* (1909-12). The *Dictionary* gathered resonance as the century wore on. It anticipated a range of effects, from the misogynist wit of *New Yorker* cartoons and the cracks of Groucho Marx to the savage satirical styles of Georg Grosz, Steve Bell and Ralph Steadman, who aptly illustrates this volume.

Collection of works suggests that their author may sense that no more of importance will follow. Bierce may have felt written, talked and drunken out. By the autumn of 1913, he was talking about going to Mexico to witness the revolution in progress there, as if it might be form of euthanasia. (To fight for Pancho Villa's rebels? To be killed as a bystander by a stray shot?) Yet he also put it to people simply that war retained its fascination for him. (So new 'works' might result?) We know that in October he toured his old Civil War battle-grounds, including Chickamauga, and that, arriving in Texas, he sent letters thence. Whether the letter received by his secretary/companion Carrie Christianson as from Chihuahua, Mexico, written December 26, was actually posted there cannot be confirmed. It was the last trace of Bierce. What is certain is that none of the numerous US journalists covering Villa's insurgence spotted that *doyen* of their craft, and that research into Bierce's disappearance launched by the US Government yielded no results whatsoever. There is likewise not a scrap of evidence to support the theory that Bierce actually headed north to Grand Canyon, found a remote spot, and shot himself.

Ambrose Bierce, *The Devil's Dictionary*, ed. Ernest Jerome Hopkins, Gollancz, London, 1967; Ambrose Bierce, *The Devil's Dictionary*, introduction by Roy Morris Jr., Oxford University Press, Oxford, 1999; Ambrose Bierce, *Tales of Soldiers and Civilians and Other Stories*, ed. Tom Quirk, Penguin, New York, London, 2000; Roy Morris Jr., *Ambrose Bierce: Alone in Bad Company*, Oxford University Press, Oxford, 1995; Richard O'Connor, *Ambrose Bierce: A Biography*, Gollancz, London, 1968.

PUBLISHER'S NOTE

The text of this edition has been abridged from that published in Volume 7 (1911) of Ambrose Bierce: *Collected Works* (1909-12).

Abasement, *n.* A decent and customary mental attitude in the presence of wealth or power. Peculiarly appropriate in an employee when addressing an employer.

Abatis, *n.* Rubbish in front of a fort, to prevent the rubbish outside from molesting the rubbish inside.

Abdication, *n.* An act whereby a sovereign attests his sense of the high temperature of the throne.

Abdomen, *n.* The temple of the god Stomach, in whose worship, with sacrificial rights, all true men engage. From women this ancient faith commands but a stammering assent. They sometimes minister at the altar in a half-hearted and ineffective way, but true reverence for the one deity that men really adore they know not. If woman had a free hand in the world's marketing the race would become graminivorous.

Ability, *n.* The natural equipment to accomplish some small part of the meaner ambitions distinguishing able men from dead ones. In the last analysis ability is commonly found to consist mainly in a high degree of solemnity. Perhaps, however, this impressive quality is rightly appraised; it is no easy task to be solemn.

Abnormal, *adj.* Not conforming to standard. In matters of thought and conduct, to be independent is to be abnormal, to be abnormal is to be detested. Wherefore the lexicographer adviseth a striving toward a straiter resemblance to the Average Man than he hath to himself. Whoso attaineth thereto shall have peace, the prospect of death and the hope of Hell.

Aborigines, *n.* Persons of little worth found cumbering the soil of a newly discovered country. They soon cease to cumber; they fertilize.

Abrupt, *adj.* Sudden, without ceremony, like the arrival of a cannonshot and the departure of the soldier whose interests are most affected by it. Dr Samuel Johnson beautifully said of another author's ideas that they were 'concatenated without abruption.'

Abscond, *v.i.* To 'move in a mysterious way,' commonly with the property of another.

Absentee, *n.* A person with an income who has had

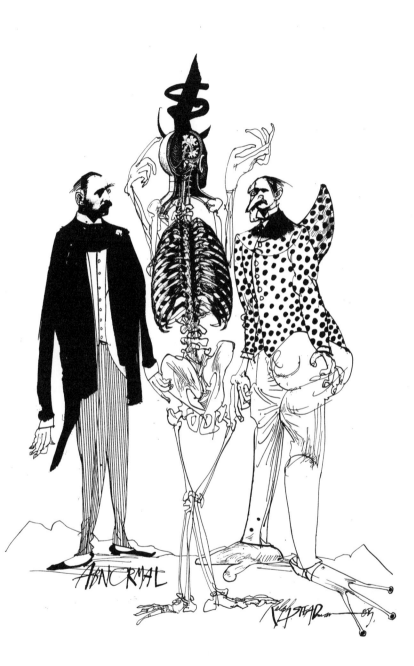

the forethought to remove himself from the sphere of exaction.

Absolute, *adj.* Independent, irresponsible. An absolute monarchy is one in which the sovereign does as he pleases so long as he pleases the assassins. Not many absolute monarchies are left, most of them having been replaced by limited monarchies, where the sovereign's power for evil (and for good) is greatly curtailed, and by republics, which are governed by chance.

Abstainer, *n.* A weak person who yields to the temptation of denying himself a pleasure. A total abstainer is one who abstains from everything but abstention, and especially from inactivity in the affairs of others.

Absurdity, *n.* A statement of belief manifestly inconsistent with one's own opinion.

Academe, *n.* An ancient school where morality and philosophy were taught.

Academy, *n.* (from academe). A modern school where football is taught.

Accident, *n.* An inevitable occurrence due to the action of immutable natural laws.

Accomplice, *n.* One associated with another in a crime, having guilty knowledge and complicity, as an attorney who defends a criminal, knowing him guilty. This view of the attorney's position in the matter has not hitherto commanded the assent of attorneys, no one having offered them a fee for assenting.

Accord, *n.* Harmony.

Accordion, *n.* An instrument in harmony with the sentiments of an assassin.

Accountability, *n.* The mother of caution.

Accuse, *v.t.* To affirm another's guilt or unworth; most commonly as a justification of ourselves for having wronged him.

Achievement, *n.* The death of endeavor and the birth of disgust.

Acknowledge, *v.t.* To confess. Acknowledgment of one another's faults is the highest duty imposed by our love of truth.

Acquaintance, *n.* A person whom we know well enough to borrow from, but not well enough to lend to. A degree of friendship called slight when its object is poor or obscure, and intimate when he is rich or famous.

Actually, *adv.* Perhaps; possibly.

Adage, *n.* Boned wisdom for weak teeth.

Adamant, *n.* A mineral frequently found beneath a corset. Soluble in solicitate of gold.

Adder, *n.* A species of snake. So called from its habit of adding funeral outlays to the other expenses of living.

Adherent, *n.* A follower who has not yet obtained all that he expects to get.

Administration, *n.* An ingenious abstraction in politics, designed to receive the kicks and cuffs due to the premier or president.

Admiral, *n.* That part of a warship which does the talking while the figurehead does the thinking.

Admiration, *n.* Our polite recognition of another's resemblance to ourselves.

Admonition, *n.* Gentle reproof, as with a meat-axe. Friendly warning.

Adore, *v.t.* To venerate expectantly.

Advice, *n.* The smallest current coin.

Affianced, *pp.* Fitted with an ankle-ring for the ball-and-chain.

Affliction, *n.* An acclimatizing process preparing the soul for another and bitter world.

Age, *n.* That period of life in which we compound for the vices that we still cherish by reviling those that we have no longer the enterprise to commit.

Agitator, *n.* A statesman who shakes the fruit trees of his neighbors – to dislodge the worms.

Aim, *n.* The task we set our wishes to.

Air, *n.* A nutritious substance supplied by a bountiful Providence for the fattening of the poor.

Alderman, *n.* An ingenious criminal who covers his secret thieving with a pretence of open marauding.

Alien, *n.* An American sovereign in his probationary state.

Allah, *n.* The Mahometan Supreme Being, as distinguished from the Christian, Jewish, and so forth.

Alliance, *n.* In international politics, the union of two thieves who have their hands so deeply inserted in each other's pocket that they cannot separately plunder a third.

Alligator, *n.* The crocodile of America, superior in every detail to the crocodile of the effete monarchies of the Old World.

Alone, *adj.* In bad company.

Ambidextrous, *adj.* Able to pick with equal skill a right-hand pocket or a left.

Ambition, *n.* An overmastering desire to be vilified by enemies while living and made ridiculous by friends when dead.

Amnesty, *n.* The state's magnanimity to those offenders whom it would be too expensive to punish.

Anoint, *v.t.* To grease a king or other great functionary already sufficiently slippery.

Antipathy, *n.* The sentiment inspired by one's friend's friend.

Aphorism, *n.* Predigested wisdom.

Apologize, *v.i.* To lay the foundation for a future offence.

Apostate, *n.* A leech who, having penetrated the shell of a turtle only to find that the creature has long been dead, deems it expedient to form a new attachment to a fresh turtle.

Appeal, *v.t.* In law, to put the dice into the box for another throw.

Appetite, *n.* An instinct thoughtfully implanted by Providence as a solution to the labor question.

Applause, *n.* The echo of a platitude.

Archbishop, *n.* An ecclesiastical dignitary one point holier than a bishop.

Architect, *n.* One who drafts a plan of your house, and plans a draft of your money.

Ardor, *n.* The quality that distinguishes love without knowledge.

Arena, *n.* In politics, an imaginary rat-pit in which the statesman wrestles with his record.

Aristocracy, *n.* Government by the best men. (In this sense the word is obsolete; so is that kind of government.)

Fellows that wear downy hats and clean shirts — guilty of education and suspected of bank accounts.

Armor, *n.* The kind of clothing worn by a man whose tailor is a blacksmith.

Arrayed, *pp.* Drawn up and given an orderly disposition, as a rioter hanged to a lamp-post.

Arrest, *v.t.* Formally to detain one accused of unusualness.

Artlessness, *n.* A certain engaging quality to which women attain by long study and severe practice upon the admiring male, who is pleased to fancy it resembles the candid simplicity of his young.

Asperse, *v.t.* Maliciously to ascribe to another vicious actions which one has not had the temptation and opportunity to commit.

Auctioneer, *n.* The man who proclaims with a hammer that he has picked a pocket with his tongue.

Babe or **Baby,** *n.* A misshapen creature of no particular age, sex, or condition, chiefly remarkable for the violence of the sympathies and antipathies it excites in others, itself without sentiment or emotion.

Bacchus, *n.* A convenient deity invented by the ancients as an excuse for getting drunk.

Back, *n.* That part of your friend which it is your privilege to contemplate in your adversity.

Backbite, *v.t.* To speak of a man as you find him when he can't find you.

Bait, *n.* A preparation that renders the hook more palatable. The best kind is beauty.

Baptism, *n.* A sacred rite of such efficacy that he who finds himself in heaven without having undergone it will be unhappy forever. It is performed with water in two ways – by immersion, or plunging, and by aspersion, or sprinkling.

Barometer, *n.* An ingenious instrument which indicates what kind of weather we are having.

Barrack, *n.* A house in which soldiers enjoy a portion of that of which it is their business to deprive others.

Bath, *n.* A kind of mystic ceremony substituted for religious worship, with what spiritual efficacy has not been determined.

Battle, *n.* A method of untying with the teeth a political knot that would not yield to the tongue.

Beard, *n.* The hair that is commonly cut off by those who justly execrate the absurd Chinese custom of shaving the head.

Beauty, *n.* The power by which a woman charms a lover and terrifies a husband.

Befriend, *v.t.* To make an ingrate.

Beg, *v.* To ask for something with an earnestness proportioned to the belief that it will not be given.

Beggar, *n.* One who has relied on the assistance of his friends.

Behavior, *n.* Conduct, as determined, not by principle, but by breeding.

Belladonna, *n.* In Italian a beautiful lady; in English a deadly poison. A striking example of the essential identity of the two tongues.

Benefactor, *n.* One who makes heavy purchases of ingratitude, without, however, materially affecting the price, which is still within the means of all.

Bigamy, *n.* A mistake in taste for which the wisdom of the future will adjudge a punishment called trigamy.

Bigot, *n.* One who is obstinately and zealously attached to an opinion that you do not entertain.

Billingsgate, *n.* The invective of an opponent.

Birth, *n.* The first and direst of all disasters.

Blackguard, *n.* A man whose qualities, prepared for display like a box of berries in a market – the fine ones on top – have been opened on the wrong side. An inverted gentleman.

Blank-verse, *n.* Unrhymed iambic pentameters – the most difficult kind of English verse to write acceptably; a kind, therefore, much affected by those who cannot acceptably write any kind.

Body-snatcher, *n.* A robber of grave-worms. One who supplies the young physicians with that with which the old physicians have supplied the undertaker. The hyena.

Darleeenz

Belladonna

Bondsman, *n.* A fool who, having property of his own, undertakes to become responsible for that entrusted by another to a third.

Bore, *n.* A person who talks when you wish him to listen.

Botany, *n.* The science of vegetables – those that are not good to eat, as well as those that are. It deals largely with their flowers, which are commonly badly designed, inartistic in color, and ill-smelling.

Boundary, *n.* In political geography, an imaginary line between two nations, separating the imaginary rights of one from the imaginary rights of the other.

Bounty, *n.* The liberality of one who has much, in permitting one who has nothing to get all that he can.

Brain, *n.* An apparatus with which we think that we think.

Brandy, *n.* A cordial composed of one part thunder-and-lightning, one part remorse, two parts bloody murder, one part death-hell-and-the-grave and four parts clarified Satan. Dose, a headful all the time. Brandy is said by Dr Johnson to be the drink of heroes. Only a hero will venture to drink it.

Bride, *n.* A woman with a fine prospect of happiness behind her.

Brute, *n.* See HUSBAND.

Cabbage, *n.* A familiar kitchen-garden vegetable about as large and wise as a man's head.

The cabbage is so called from Cabagius, a prince who on ascending the throne issued a decree appointing a High Council of Empire consisting of the members of his predecessor's Ministry and the cabbages in the royal garden. When any of his Majesty's measures of state policy miscarried conspicuously it was gravely announced that several members of the High Council had been beheaded, and his murmuring subjects were appeased.

Calamity, *n.* A more than commonly plain and unmistakable reminder that the affairs of this life are not of our own ordering. Calamities are of two kinds: misfortune to ourselves, and good fortune to others.

Callous, *adj.* Gifted with great fortitude to bear the evils afflicting another.

Cannibal, *n.* A gastronome of the old school who preserves the simple tastes and adheres to the natural diet of the pre-pork period.

Cannon, *n.* An instrument employed in the rectification of national boundaries.

Capital, *n.* The seat of misgovernment.

Carnivorous, *adj.* Addicted to the cruelty of devouring the timorous vegetarian, his heirs and assigns.

Cartesian, *adj.* Relating to Descartes, a famous philosopher, author of the celebrated dictum, *Cogito ergo sum* — whereby he was pleased to suppose he demonstrated the reality of human existence. The dictum might be improved, however, thus: *Cogito cogito ergo cogito sum* — 'I think that I think, therefore I think that I am'; as close an approach to certainty as any philosopher has yet made.

Cat, *n.* A soft, indestructible automaton provided by nature to be kicked when things go wrong in the domestic circle.

Caviler, *n.* A critic of our own work.

Cemetery, *n.* An isolated suburban spot where mourners match lies, poets write at a target and stone-cutters spell for a wager.

Centaur, *n.* One of a race of persons who lived before the division of labor had been carried to such a pitch of differentiation, and who followed the primitive economic maxim, 'Every man his own horse.' The best of the lot was Chiron, who to the wisdom and virtues of the horse added the fleetness of man.

Cerberus, *n.* The watch-dog of Hades, whose duty it was to guard the entrance – against whom or what does not clearly appear; everybody, sooner or later, had to go there, and nobody wanted to carry off the entrance.

Childhood, *n.* The period of human life intermediate between the idiocy of infancy and the folly of youth – two removes from the sin of manhood and three from the remorse of age.

Christian, *n.* One who believes that the New Testament is a divinely inspired book admirably suited to the spiritual needs of his neighbor. One who follows the teachings of Christ in so far as they are not inconsistent with a life of sin.

Circus, *n.* A place where horses, ponies and elephants are permitted to see men, women and children acting the fool.

Clairvoyant, *n.* A person, commonly a woman, who has the power of seeing that which is invisible to her patron – namely, that he is a blockhead.

Clarionet, *n.* An instrument of torture operated by a person with cotton in his ears. There are two instruments that are worse than a clarionet – two clarionets.

Clergyman, *n.* A man who undertakes the management of our spiritual affairs as a method of bettering his temporal ones.

Clock, *n.* A machine of great moral value to man, allaying his concern for the future by reminding him what a lot of time remains to him.

Close-fisted, *adj.* Unduly desirous of keeping that which many meritorious persons wish to obtain.

Comfort, *n.* A state of mind produced by contemplation of a neighbor's uneasiness.

Commendation, *n.* The tribute that we pay to achievements that resemble, but do not equal, our own.

Commerce, *n.* A kind of transaction in which A plunders from B the goods of C, and for compensation B picks the pocket of D of money belonging to E.

Commonwealth, *n.* An administrative entity operated by an incalculable multitude of political parasites, logically active but fortuitously efficient.

Compromise, *n.* Such an adjustment of conflicting interests as gives each adversary the satisfaction of thinking he has got what he ought not to have, and is deprived of nothing except what was justly his due.

Compulsion, *n.* The eloquence of power.

Condole, *v.i.* To show that bereavement is a smaller evil than sympathy.

Confidant, Confidante, *n.* One entrusted by A with the secrets of B, confided by *him* to C.

Congratulation, *n.* The civility of envy.

Congress, *n.* A body of men who meet to repeal laws.

Connoisseur, *n.* A specialist who knows everything about something and nothing about anything else.

Conservative, *n.* A statesman who is enamored of existing evils, as distinguished from the Liberal, who wishes to replace them with others.

Consolation, *n.* The knowledge that a better man is more unfortunate than yourself.

Consul, *n.* In American politics, a person who having failed to secure an office from the people is given one by the Administration on condition that he leave the country.

Consult, *v.t.* To seek another's approval of a course already decided on.

Contempt, *n.* The feeling of a prudent man for an enemy who is too formidable safely to be opposed.

Controversy, *n.* A battle in which spittle or ink replaces the injurious cannonball and the inconsiderate bayonet.

Conversation, *n.* A fair for the display of the minor mental commodities, each exhibitor being too intent upon the arrangement of his own wares to observe those of his neighbor.

Coronation, *n.* The ceremony of investing a sovereign with the outward and visible signs of his divine right to be blown skyhigh with a dynamite bomb.

Corporation, *n.* An ingenious device for obtaining individual profit without individual responsibility.

Corsair, *n.* A politician of the seas.

Court Fool, *n.* The plaintiff.

Coward, *n.* One who in a perilous emergency thinks with his legs.

Craft, *n.* A fool's substitute for brains.

Crayfish, *n.* A small crustacean very much resembling the lobster, but less indigestible.

Creditor, *n.* One of a tribe of savages dwelling beyond the Financial Straits and dreaded for their desolating incursions.

Cremona, *n.* A high-priced violin made in Connecticut.

Critic, *n.* A person who boasts himself hard to please because nobody tries to please him.

Cui Bono? (Latin). What good would that do *me*?

Cunning, *n.* The faculty that distinguishes a weak animal or person from a strong one. It brings its possessor much mental satisfaction and great material adversity. An Italian proverb says: 'The furrier gets the skins of more foxes than asses.'

Cupid, *n.* The so-called god of love. This bastard creation of a barbarous fancy was no doubt inflicted upon mythology for the sins of its deities. Of all unbeautiful and inappropriate conceptions this is the most reasonless and offensive. The notion of symbolizing sexual love by a semisexless babe, and comparing the pains of passion to the wounds of an arrow – of introducing this pudgy homunculus into art grossly to materialize the subtle spirit and suggestion of the work – this is eminently worthy of the age that, giving it birth, laid it on the doorstep of posterity.

Curiosity, *n.* An objectionable quality of the female mind. The desire to know whether or not a woman is cursed with curiosity is one of the most active and insatiable passions of the masculine soul.

Curse, *v.t.* Energetically to belabor with a verbal slap-stick.

Cynic, *n.* A blackguard whose faulty vision sees things as they are, not as they ought to be. Hence the custom among the Scythians of plucking out a cynic's eyes to improve his vision.

Dance, *v.i.* To leap about to the sound of tittering music, preferably with arms about your neighbor's wife or daughter. There are many kinds of dances, but all those requiring the participation of the two sexes have two characteristics in common: they are conspicuously innocent, and warmly loved by the vicious.

Daring, *n.* One of the most conspicuous qualities of a man in security.

Dawn, *n.* The time when men of reason go to bed. Certain old men prefer to rise at about that time, taking a cold bath and a long walk with an empty stomach, and otherwise mortifying the flesh. They then point with pride to these practices as the cause of their sturdy health and ripe years; the truth being that they are hearty and old, not because of their habits, but in spite of them. The reason we find only robust persons doing this thing is that it has killed all the others who have tried it.

Day, *n.* A period of twenty-four hours, mostly misspent. This period is divided into two parts, the day proper and the night, or day improper – the former devoted to sins of business, the latter consecrated to the other sort. These two kinds of social activity overlap.

Debauchee, *n.* One who has so earnestly pursued pleasure that he has had the misfortune to overtake it.

Debt, *n.* An ingenious substitute for the chain and whip of the slave-driver.

Decalogue, *n.* A series of commandments, ten in number – just enough to permit an intelligent selection for observance, but not enough to embarrass the choice. Following is the revised edition of the Decalogue, calculated for this meridian.

> Thou shalt no God but me adore:
> 'Twere too expensive to have more.
>
> No images nor idols make
> For Robert Ingersoll to break.
>
> Take not God's name in vain; select
> A time when it will have effect.
>
> Work not on Sabbath days at all,
> But go to see the teams play ball.

Honor thy parents. That creates
For life insurance lower rates.

Kill not, abet not those who kill;
Thou shalt not pay thy butcher's bill.

Kiss not thy neighbor's wife, unless
Thine own thy neighbor doth caress.

Don't steal; thou'lt never thus compete
Successfully in business. Cheat.

Bear not false witness – that is low –
But 'hear 'tis rumored so and so.'

Covet thou naught that thou hast not
By hook or crook, or somehow, got.

Decide, *v.i.* To succumb to the preponderance of one set of influences over another set.

Defame, *v.t.* To lie about another. To tell the truth about another.

Defenceless, *adj.* Unable to attack.

Degradation, *n.* One of the stages of moral and social progress from private station to political preferment.

Dejeuner, *n.* The breakfast of an American who has been in Paris. Variously pronounced.

Delegation, *n.* In American politics, an article of merchandise that comes in sets.

Deliberation, *n.* The act of examining one's bread to determine which side it is buttered on.

Deluge, *n.* A notable first experiment in baptism which washed away the sins (and sinners) of the world.

Delusion, *n.* The father of a most respectable family, comprising Enthusiasm, Affection, Self-denial, Faith, Hope, Charity and many other goodly sons and daughters.

Dentist, *n.* A prestidigitator who, putting metal into your mouth, pulls coins out of your pocket.

Dependent, *adj.* Reliant upon another's generosity for the support which you are not in a position to exact from his fears.

Destiny, *n.* A tyrant's authority for crime and a fool's excuse for failure.

Diagnosis, *n.* A physician's forecast of disease by the patient's pulse and purse.

Diary, *n.* A daily record of that part of one's life, which he can relate to himself without blushing.

Dictator, *n.* The chief of a nation that prefers the pestilence of despotism to the plague of anarchy.

Dictionary, *n.* A malevolent literary device for cramping the growth of a language and making it hard and inelastic. This dictionary, however, is a most useful work.

Die, *n.* The singular of 'dice.' We seldom hear the word, because there is a prohibitory proverb, 'Never say die.' At long intervals, however, some one says: 'The die is cast,' which is not true, for it is cut.

Digestion, *n.* The conversion of victuals into virtues.

Diplomacy, *n.* The patriotic art of lying for one's country.

Disabuse, *v.t.* To present your neighbor with another and better error than the one which he has deemed it advantageous to embrace.

Discriminate, *v.i.* To note the particulars in which one person or thing is, if possible, more objectionable than another.

Discussion, *n.* A method of confirming others in their errors.

Disobedience, *n.* The silver lining to the cloud of servitude.

Disobey, *v.t.* To celebrate with an appropriate ceremony the maturity of a command.

Dissemble, *v.i.* To put a clean shirt upon the character.

Distance, *n.* The only thing that the rich are willing for the poor to call theirs, and keep.

Distress, *n.* A disease incurred by exposure to the prosperity of a friend.

Divination, *n.* The art of nosing out the occult. Divination is of as many kinds as there are fruit-bearing varieties of the flowering dunce and the early fool.

Dog, *n.* A kind of additional or subsidiary Deity designed to catch the overflow and surplus of the world's worship. This Divine Being in some of his smaller and silkier incarnations, takes, in the affection of Woman, the place to which there is no human male aspirant.

Dragoon, *n.* A soldier who combines dash and steadiness in so equal measure that he makes his advances on foot and his retreats on horseback.

Druids, *n.* Priests and ministers of an ancient Celtic religion which did not disdain to employ the humble allurement of human sacrifice.

Duel, *n.* A formal ceremony preliminary to the reconciliation of two enemies. Great skill is necessary to its satisfactory observance; if awkwardly performed the most unexpected and deplorable consequences sometimes ensue. A long time ago a man lost his life in a duel.

Dullard, *n.* A member of the reigning dynasty in letters and life. The Dullards came in with Adam, and being both numerous and sturdy have overrun the habitable world. The secret of their power is their insensibility to blows; tickle them with a bludgeon and they laugh with a platitude.

Duty, *n.* That which sternly impels us in the direction of profit, along the line of desire.

DOG

Eat, *v.i.* To perform successively (and successfully) the functions of mastication, humectation, and deglutition.

Eavesdrop, *v.i.* Secretly to overhear a catalogue of the crimes and vices of another or yourself.

Eccentricity, *n.* A method of distinction so cheap that fools employ it to accentuate their incapacity.

Economy, *n.* Purchasing the barrel of whiskey that you do not need for the price of the cow that you cannot afford.

Edible, *adj.* Good to eat, and wholesome to digest, as a worm to a toad, a toad to a snake, a snake to a pig, a pig to a man, and a man to a worm.

Editor, *n.* A person who combines the judicial functions of Minos, Rhadamanthus and Æacus, but is placable with an obolus; a severely virtuous censor, but so charitable withal that he tolerates the virtues of others and the vices of himself; who flings about him the splintering lightning and sturdy thunders of admonition till he resembles a bunch of firecrackers petulantly uttering its mind at the tail of a dog; then straightway murmurs a mild, melodious lay, soft as the cooing of a donkey intoning its prayer to the evening star. Master of mysteries and lord of law, high-pinnacled upon the throne of thought, his face suffused with the dim splendors of the Transfiguration, his legs intertwisted and his tongue a-cheek, the editor spills his will along the paper and cuts it off in lengths to suit. And at intervals from behind the veil of the temple is heard the voice of the foreman demanding three inches of wit and six lines of religious meditation, or bidding him turn off the wisdom and whack up some pathos.

Education, *n.* That which discloses to the wise and disguises from the foolish their lack of understanding.

Effect, *n.* The second of two phenomena which always occur together in the same order. The first, called a Cause, is said to generate the other – which is no more sensible than it would be for one who has never seen a dog except in pursuit of a rabbit to declare the rabbit the cause of the dog.

Egotist, *n.* A person of low taste, more interested in himself than in me.

Ejection, *n.* An approved remedy for the disease of garrulity. It is also much used in cases of extreme poverty.

Elector, *n.* One who enjoys the sacred privilege of voting for the man of another man's choice.

Electricity, *n.* The power that causes all natural phenomena not known to be caused by something else.

Elegy, *n.* A composition in verse, in which, without employing any of the methods of humor, the writer aims to produce in the reader's mind the dampest kind of dejection.

Eloquence, *n.* The art of orally persuading fools that white is the color that it appears to be. It includes the gift of making any color appear white.

Elysium, *n.* An imaginary delightful country which the ancients foolishly believed to be inhabited by the spirits of the good. This ridiculous and mischievous fable was swept off the face of the earth by the early Christians – may their souls be happy in Heaven!

Emancipation, *n.* A bondman's change from the tyranny of another to the despotism of himself.

Embalm, *v.t.* To cheat vegetation by locking up the gases upon which it feeds. By embalming their dead and thereby deranging the natural balance between animal and vegetable life, the Egyptians made their once fertile and populous country barren and incapable of supporting more than a meagre crew. The modern metallic burial casket is a step in the same direction, and many a dead man who ought now to be ornamenting his neighbor's lawn as a tree, or enriching his table as a bunch of radishes, is doomed to a long inutility. We shall get him after a while if we are spared, but in the meantime the violet and rose are languishing for a nibble at his *glutæus maximus*.

Emotion, *n.* A prostrating disease caused by a determination of the heart to the head. It is sometimes accompanied by a copious discharge of hydrated chloride of sodium from the eyes.

Encomiast, *n.* A special (but not particular) kind of liar.

Entertainment, *n.* Any kind of amusement whose inroads stop short of death by dejection.

Enthusiasm, *n.* A distemper of youth, curable by small doses of repentance in connection with outward applications of experience.

Envy, *n.* Emulation adapted to the meanest capacity.

Epaulet, *n.* An ornamented badge, serving to distinguish a military officer from the enemy – that is to say, from the officer of the lower rank to whom his death would give promotion.

Epicure, *n.* An opponent of Epicurus, an abstemious philosopher who, holding that pleasure should be the chief aim of man, wasted no time in gratification of the senses.

Epigram, *n.* A short, sharp saying in prose or verse, frequently characterized by acidity or acerbity and sometimes by wisdom. Following are some of the more notable epigrams of the learned and ingenious Dr Jamrach Holobom:

> We know better the needs of ourselves than of others. To serve oneself is economy of administration.

> In each human heart are a tiger, a pig, an ass and a nightingale. Diversity of character is due to their unequal activity.

> There are three sexes; males, females and girls.

> Beauty in women and distinction in men are alike in this: they seem to the unthinking a kind of credibility.

> Women in love are less ashamed than men. They have less to be ashamed of.

> While your friend holds you affectionately by both your hands you are safe, for you can watch both his.

Epitaph, *n.* An inscription on a tomb, showing that virtues acquired by death have a retroactive effect.

Erudition, *n.* Dust shaken out of a book into an empty skull.

Esoteric, *adj.* Very particularly abstruse and consummately occult. The ancient philosophies were of two kinds, – *exoteric*, those that the philosophers themselves could partly understand, and *esoteric*, those that nobody could understand. It is the latter that have most profoundly affected modern thought and found greatest acceptance in our time.

Ethnology, *n.* The science that treats of the various tribes of Man, as robbers, thieves, swindlers, dunces, lunatics, idiots and ethnologists.

Eulogy, *n.* Praise of a person who has either the advantages of wealth and power, or the consideration to be dead.

Evangelist, *n.* A bearer of good tidings, particularly (in a religious sense) such as assure us of our own salvation and the damnation of our neighbors.

Exception, *n.* A thing which takes the liberty to differ from other things of its class, as an honest man, a truthful woman, etc. 'The exception proves the rule' is an expression constantly upon the lips of the ignorant, who parrot it from one another with never a thought of its absurdity. In the Latin, '*Exceptio probat regulam*' means that the exception *tests* the rule, puts it to the proof, not *confirms* it. The malefactor who drew the meaning from this excellent dictum and substituted a contrary one of his own exerted an evil power which appears to be immortal.

Excess, *n.* In morals, an indulgence that enforces by appropriate penalties the law of moderation.

Executive, *n.* An officer of the Government, whose duty it is to enforce the wishes of the legislative power until such time as the judicial department shall be pleased to pronounce them invalid and of no effect.

Exhort, *v.t.* In religious affairs, to put the conscience of another upon the spit and roast it to a nut-brown discomfort.

Exile, *n.* One who serves his country by residing abroad, yet is not an ambassador.

Experience, *n.* The wisdom that enables us to recognize as an undesirable old acquaintance the folly that we have already embraced.

Expostulation, *n.* One of the many methods by which fools prefer to lose their friends.

Extinction, *n.* The raw material out of which theology created the future state.

Faith, *n.* Belief without evidence in what is told by one who speaks without knowledge, of things without parallel.

Famous, *adj.* Conspicuously miserable.

Fashion, *n.* A despot whom the wise ridicule and obey.

Feast, *n.* A festival. A religious celebration usually signalized by gluttony and drunkenness, frequently in honor of some holy person distinguished for abstemiousness.

Felon, *n.* A person of greater enterprise than discretion, who in embracing an opportunity has formed an unfortunate attachment.

Female, *n.* One of the opposing, or unfair, sex.

Fib, *n.* A lie that has not cut its teeth. An habitual liar's nearest approach to truth: the perigee of his eccentric orbit.

Fickleness, *n.* The iterated satiety of an enterprising affection.

Fiddle, *n.* An instrument to tickle human ears by friction of a horse's tail on the entrails of a cat.

Fidelity, *n.* A virtue peculiar to those who are about to be betrayed.

Finance, *n.* The art or science of managing revenues and resources for the best advantage of the manager. The pronunciation of this word with the i long and the accent on the first syllable is one of America's most precious discoveries and possessions.

Flag, *n.* A colored rag borne above troops and hoisted on forts and ships. It appears to serve the same purpose as certain signs that one sees on vacant lots in London – 'Rubbish may be shot here.'

Flesh, *n.* The Second Person of the secular Trinity.

Flop, *v.* Suddenly to change one's opinions and go over to another party. The most notable flop on record was that of Saul of Tarsus, who has been severely criticized as a turn-coat by some of our partisan journals.

Folly, *n.* That 'gift and faculty divine' whose creative and controlling energy inspires Man's mind, guides his actions and adorns his life.

Fool, *n.* A person who pervades the domain of intellectual speculation and diffuses himself through the channels of moral activity. He is omnific, omniform, omnipercipient, omniscient, omnipotent. He it was who invented letters, printing, the railroad, the steamboat, the telegraph, the platitude, and the circle of the sciences. He created patriotism and taught the nations war – founded theology, philosophy, law, medicine and Chicago. He established monarchical and republican government. He is from everlasting to everlasting – such as creation's dawn beheld he fooleth now. In the morning of time he sang upon primitive hills, and in the noonday of existence headed the procession of being. His grandmotherly hand has warmly tucked in the set sun of civilization, and in the twilight he prepares Man's evening meal of milk-and-morality and turns down the covers of the universal grave. And after the rest of us shall have retired for the night of eternal oblivion he will sit up to write a history of human civilization.

Forefinger, *n.* The finger commonly used in pointing out two malefactors.

Forgetfulness, *n.* A gift of God bestowed upon debtors in compensation for their destitution of conscience.

Fork, *n.* An instrument used chiefly for the purpose of putting dead animals into the mouth.

Freebooter, *n.* A conqueror in a small way of business, whose annexations lack the sanctifying merit of magnitude.

Freedom, *n.* Exemption from the stress of authority in a beggarly half dozen of restraint's infinite multitude of methods. A political condition that every nation supposes itself to enjoy in virtual monopoly. Liberty. The distinction between freedom and liberty is not accurately known; naturalists have never been able to find a living specimen of either.

Freemasons, *n.* An order with secret rites, grotesque ceremonies and fantastic costumes, which, originating in the reign of Charles II, among working artisans of London, has been joined successively by the dead of past centuries in unbroken retrogression until now it embraces all the generations of man on the hither side of Adam and is drumming up distinguished recruits among the pre-Creational inhabitants of Chaos and the Formless Void. The order was founded at different times by Charlemagne, Julius Cæsar, Cyrus, Solomon, Zoroaster, Confucius, Thothmes, and Buddha. Its emblems and symbols have been found in the Catacombs of Paris and Rome, on the stones of the Parthenon and the Chinese Great Wall, among the temples of Karnak and Palmyra and in the Egyptian Pyramids – always by a Freemason.

Friendless, *adj.* Having no favors to bestow. Destitute of fortune. Addicted to utterance of truth and common sense.

Friendship, *n.* A ship big enough to carry two in fair weather, but only one in foul.

Frog, *n.* A reptile with edible legs.

Funeral, *n.* A pageant whereby we attest our respect for the dead by enriching the undertaker, and strengthen our grief by an expenditure that deepens our groans and doubles our tears.

Future, *n.* That period of time in which our affairs prosper, our friends are true and our happiness is assured.

Generous, *adj.* Originally this word meant noble by birth and was rightly applied to a great multitude of persons. It now means noble by nature and is taking a bit of a rest.

Genealogy, *n.* An account of one's descent from an ancestor who did not particularly care to trace his own.

Genteel, *adj.* Refined, after the fashion of a gent.

Geographer, *n.* A chap who can tell you offhand the difference between the outside of the world and the inside.

Geology, *n.* The science of the earth's crust – to which, doubtless, will be added that of its interior whenever a man shall come up garrulous out of a well. The geological formations of the globe already noted are catalogued thus: The Primary, or lower one, consists of rocks, bones of mired mules, gas-pipes, miners' tools, antique statues minus the nose, Spanish doubloons and ancestors. The Secondary is largely made up of red worms and moles. The Tertiary comprises railway tracks, patent pavements, grass, snakes, mouldy boots, beer bottles, tomato cans, intoxicated citizens, garbage, anarchists, snap-dogs and fools.

Ghost, *n.* The outward and visible sign of an inward fear.

Ghoul, *n.* A demon addicted to the reprehensible habit of devouring the dead. The existence of ghouls has been disputed by that class of controversialists who are more concerned to deprive the world of comforting beliefs than to give it anything good in their place.

Glutton, *n.* A person who escapes the evils of moderation by committing dyspepsia.

Gnome, *n.* In North-European mythology, a dwarfish imp inhabiting the interior parts of the earth and having special custody of mineral treasures. Bjorsen, who died in 1765, says gnomes were common enough in the southern parts of Sweden in his boyhood, and he frequently saw them scampering on the hills in the evening twilight. Ludwig Binkerhoof saw three as recently as 1792 in the Black Forest, and Sneddeker avers that in 1803 they drove a party of miners out of a Silesian mine. Basing our computations upon data supplied by these statements, we find that gnomes were probably extinct as early as 1764.

Gnu, *n.* An animal of South Africa, which in its domesticated state resembles a horse, a buffalo and a stag. In its wild condition it is something like a thunderbolt, an earthquake and a cyclone.

Good, *adj.* Sensible, madam, to the worth of this present writer. Alive, sir, to the advantages of letting him alone.

Gout, *n.* A physician's name for the rheumatism of a rich patient.

Grammar, *n.* A system of pitfalls thoughtfully prepared for the feet of the self-made man, along the path by which he advances to distinction.

Grave, *n.* A place in which the dead are laid to await the coming of the medical student.

Guillotine, *n.* A machine which makes a Frenchman shrug his shoulders with good reason.

Gunpowder, *n.* An agency employed by civilized nations for the settlement of disputes which might become troublesome if left unadjusted. By most writers the invention of gunpowder is ascribed to the Chinese, but not upon very convincing evidence. Milton says it was invented by the devil to dispel angels with, and this opinion seems to derive some support from the scarcity of angels.

Habeas Corpus. A writ by which a man may be taken out of jail when confined for the wrong crime.

Habit, *n.* A shackle for the free.

Hades, *n.* The lower world; the residence of departed spirits; the place where the dead live.

Among the ancients the idea of Hades was not synonymous with our Hell, many of the most respectable men of antiquity residing there in a very comfortable kind of way. Indeed, the Elysian Fields themselves were a part of Hades, though they have since been removed to Paris. When the Jacobean version of the New Testament was in process of evolution the pious and learned men engaged in the work insisted by a majority vote on translating the Greek word Αιδης as 'Hell'; but a conscientious minority member secretly possessed himself of the record and struck out the objectionable word wherever he could find it. At the next meeting, the Bishop of Salisbury, looking over the work, suddenly sprang to his feet and said with considerable excitement: 'Gentlemen, somebody has been razing "Hell" here!' Years afterward the good prelate's death was made sweet by the reflection that he had been the means (under Providence) of making an important, serviceable and immortal addition to the phraseology of the English tongue.

Hag, *n.* An elderly lady whom you do not happen to like; sometimes called, also, a hen, or cat. Old witches, sorceresses, etc., were called hags from the belief that their heads were surrounded by a kind of baleful lumination or nimbus – hag being the popular name of that peculiar electrical light sometimes observed in the hair. At one time hag was not a word of reproach: Drayton speaks of a 'beautiful hag, all smiles,' much as Shakespeare said, 'sweet wench.' It would not now be proper to call your sweetheart a hag – that compliment is reserved for the use of her grandchildren.

Hand, *n.* A singular instrument worn at the end of a human arm and commonly thrust into somebody's pocket.

Handkerchief, *n.* A small square of silk or linen, used in various ignoble offices about the face and especially serviceable at funerals to conceal the lack of tears.

THINGS TO DO WHEN YOU'RE OLD. Nº 1

Hangman, *n.* An officer of the law charged with duties of the highest dignity and utmost gravity, and held in hereditary disesteem by a populace having a criminal ancestry. In some of the American States his functions are now performed by an electrician.

Happiness, *n.* An agreeable sensation arising from contemplating the misery of another.

Harangue, *n.* A speech by an opponent, who is known as an harangue-outang.

Harbor, *n.* A place where ships taking shelter from storms are exposed to the fury of the customs.

Hash, *x.* There is no definition for this word – nobody knows what hash is.

Hatred, *n.* A sentiment appropriate to the occasion of another's superiority.

Head-money, *n.* A capitation tax, or poll-tax.

Hearse, *n.* Death's baby-carriage.

Heart, *n.* An automatic, muscular blood-pump. Figuratively, this useful organ is said to be the seat of emotions and sentiments – a very pretty fancy which, however, is nothing but a survival of a once universal belief. It is now known that the sentiments and emotions reside in the stomach, being evolved from food by chemical action of the gastric fluid.

Heathen, *n.* A benighted creature who has the folly to worship something that he can see and feel.

Heaven, *n.* A place where the wicked cease from troubling you with talk of their personal affairs, and the good listen with attention while you expound your own.

Helpmate, *n.* A wife, or bitter half.

Hermit, *n.* A person whose vices and follies are not sociable.

Hers, *pron.* His.

Hibernate, *v.i.* To pass the winter season in domestic seclusion. There have been many singular popular notions about the hibernation of various animals. Many believe that the bear hibernates during the whole winter and subsists by mechanically sucking its paws. It is admitted that it comes out of its retirement in the spring so lean that it has to try twice before it can cast a shadow.

Hippogriff, *n.* An animal (now extinct) which was half horse and half griffin. The griffin was itself a compound creature, half lion and half eagle. The hippogriff was actually, therefore, only one-quarter eagle, which is two dollars and fifty cents in gold. The study of zoology is full of surprises.

Historian, *n.* A broad-gauge gossip.

History, *n.* An account mostly false, of events mostly unimportant, which are brought about by rulers mostly knaves, and soldiers mostly fools.

Homœopathist, *n.* The humorist of the medical profession.

Homœopathy, *n.* A school of medicine midway between Allopathy and Christian Science. To the last both the others are distinctly inferior, for Christian Science will cure imaginary diseases, and they cannot.

Homicide, *n.* The slaying of one human being by another. There are four kinds of homicide: felonious, excusable, justifiable and praiseworthy, but it makes no great difference to the person slain whether he fell by one kind or another – the classification is for advantage of the lawyers.

Honorable, *adj.* Afflicted with an impediment in one's reach. In legislative bodies it is customary to mention all members as honorable; as, 'the honorable gentleman is a scurvy cur.'

Hope, *n.* Desire and expectation rolled into one.

Hospitality, *n.* The virtue which induces us to feed and lodge certain persons who are not in need of food and lodging.

Hostility, *n.* A peculiarly sharp and specially applied sense of the earth's over-population. Hostility is classed as active and passive; as (respectively) the feeling of a woman for her female friends, and that which she entertains for all the rest of her sex.

House, *n.* A hollow edifice erected for the habitation of man, rat, mouse, beetle, cockroach, fly, mosquito, flea, bacillus and microbe.

Houseless, *adj.* Having paid all taxes on household goods.

Humanity, *n.* The human race, collectively, exclusive of the anthropoid poets.

Hurricane, *n.* An atmospheric demonstration once very common but now generally abandoned for the tornado and cyclone. The hurricane is still in popular use in the West Indies and is preferred by certain old-fashioned sea-captains. It is also used in the construction of the upper decks of steamboats, but generally speaking, the hurricane's usefulness has outlasted it.

Hurry, *n.* The dispatch of bunglers.

Husband, *n.* One who, having dined, is charged with the care of the plate.

Hybrid, *n.* A pooled issue.

Hydra, *n.* A kind of animal that the ancients catalogued under many heads.

Hypocrite, *n.* One who, professing virtues that he does not respect, secures the advantage of seeming to be what he despises.

Iconoclast, *n.* A breaker of idols, the worshipers whereof are imperfectly gratified by the performance, and most strenuously protest that he unbuildeth but doth not re-edify, that he pulleth down but pileth not up. For the poor things would have other idols in place of those he thwacketh upon the mazzard and dispelleth. But the iconoclast saith: 'Ye shall have none at all, for ye need them not; and if the rebuilder fooleth round hereabout, behold I will depress the head of him and sit thereon till he squawk it.'

Idiot, *n.* A member of a large and powerful tribe whose influence in human affairs has always been dominant and controlling. The Idiot's activity is not confined to any special field of thought or action, but 'pervades and regulates the whole.' He has the last word in everything; his decision is unappealable. He sets the fashions of opinion and taste, dictates the limitations of speech and circumscribes conduct with a dead-line.

Idleness, *n.* A model farm where the Devil experiments with seeds of new sins and promotes the growth of staple vices.

Ignoramus, *n.* A person unacquainted with certain kinds of knowledge familiar to yourself, and having certain other kinds that you know nothing about.

Illuminati, *n.* A sect of Spanish heretics of the latter part of the sixteenth century; so called because they were light weights – *cunctationes illuminati.*

Illustrious, *adj.* Suitably placed for the shafts of malice, envy and detraction.

Imagination, *n.* A warehouse of facts, with poet and liar in joint ownership.

Imbecility, *n.* A kind of divine inspiration, or sacred fire affecting censorious critics of this dictionary.

Immigrant, *n.* An unenlightened person who thinks one country better than another.

Immodest, *adj.* Having a strong sense of one's own merit, coupled with a feeble conception of worth in others.

Immoral, *adj.* Inexpedient. Whatever in the long run and

with regard to the greater number of instances men find
to be generally inexpedient comes to be considered
wrong, wicked, immoral. If man's notions of right and
wrong have any other basis than this of expediency; if
they originated, or could have originated, in any other
way; if actions have in themselves a moral character apart
from and nowise dependent on, their consequences – then
all philosophy is a lie and reason a disorder of the mind.

Immortality, *n.*

> A toy which people cry for,
> And on their knees apply for,
> Dispute, contend and lie for,
>> And if allowed
>> Would be right proud
> Eternally to die for.

Impartial, *adj.* Unable to perceive any promise of
personal advantage from espousing either side of a controversy or adopting either of two conflicting opinions.

Impenitence, *n.* A state of mind intermediate in point
of time between sin and punishment.

Impiety, *n.* Your irreverence toward my deity.

Imposition, *n.* The act of blessing or consecrating by the
laying on of hands – a ceremony common to many ecclesiastical systems, but performed with the frankest sincerity
by the sect known as Thieves.

Impostor, *n.* A rival aspirant to public honors.

Improvidence, *n.* Provision for the needs of today from the revenues of tomorrow.

Impunity, *n.* Wealth.

Inadmissible, *adj.* Not competent to be considered. Said of certain kinds of testimony which juries are supposed to be unfit to be entrusted with, and which judges, therefore, rule out, even of proceedings before themselves alone. Hearsay evidence is inadmissible because the person quoted was unsworn and is not before the court for examination; yet most momentous actions, military, political, commercial and of every other kind, are daily undertaken on hearsay evidence. There is no religion in the world that has any other basis than hearsay evidence. Revelation is hearsay evidence; that the Scriptures are the word of God we have only the testimony of men long dead whose identity is not clearly established and who are not known to have been sworn in any sense. Under the rules of evidence as they now exist in this country, no single assertion in the Bible has in its support any evidence admissible in a court of law. It cannot be proved that the battle of Blenheim ever was fought, that there was such a person as Julius Cæsar, such an empire as Assyria.

But as records of courts of justice are admissible, it can easily be proved that powerful and malevolent magicians once existed and were a scourge to mankind. The evidence (including confession) upon which certain women were convicted of witchcraft and executed was without a flaw; it is still unimpeachable. The judges' decisions based on it were sound in logic and in law. Nothing in any existing court was ever more thoroughly proved than the charges of witchcraft and sorcery for which so many suffered death. If there were no witches, human testimony and human reason are alike destitute of value.

Inauspiciously, *adv.* In an unpromising manner, the auspices being unfavorable. Among the Romans it was customary before undertaking any important action or enterprise to obtain from the augurs, or state prophets, some hint of its probable outcome; and one of their favorite and most trustworthy modes of divination consisted in observing the flight of birds – the omens thence derived being called *auspices*. Newspaper reporters and certain miscreant lexicographers have decided that the word – always in the plural – shall mean 'patronage' or 'management'; as, 'The festivities were under the auspices of the Ancient and Honorable Order of Body-Snatchers'; or, 'The hilarities were auspicated by the Knights of Hunger.'

Incompatibility, *n.* In matrimony a similarity of tastes, particularly the taste for domination. Incompatibility may, however, consist of a meek-eyed matron living just around the corner. It has even been known to wear a moustache.

Incompossible, *adj.* Unable to exist if something else exists. Two things are incompossible when the world of being has scope enough for one of them, but not enough for both – as Walt Whitman's poetry and God's mercy to man. Incompossibility, it will be seen, is only incompatibility let loose.

Incubus, *n.* One of a race of highly improper demons who, though probably not wholly extinct, may be said to have seen their best nights. For a complete account of *incubi* and *succubi*, including *incubœ*, and *succubœ*, see the *Liber Demonorum* of Protassus (Paris, 1328), which contains much curious information that would be out of place in a dictionary intended as a text-book for the public schools.

Incumbent, *n.* A person of the liveliest interest to the outcumbents.

Indecision, *n.* The chief element of success; 'for whereas,' said Sir Thomas Brewbold, 'there is but one way to do nothing and divers ways to do something, whereof, to a surety, only one is the right way, it followeth that he who from indecision standeth still hath not so many chances of going astray as he who pusheth forwards' – a most clear and satisfactory exposition of the matter.

Indifferent, *adj.* Imperfectly sensible to distinctions among things.

Indiscretion, *n.* The guilt of woman.

Inexpedient, *adj.* Not calculated to advance one's interests.

Infancy, *n.* The period of our lives when, according to Wordsworth, 'Heaven lies about us.' The world begins lying about us pretty soon afterward.

Infidel, *n.* In New York, one who does not believe in the Christian religion; in Constantinople, one who does.

A kind of scoundrel imperfectly reverent of, and niggardly contributory to, divines, ecclesiastics, popes, parsons, canons, monks, mollahs, voodoos, presbyters, hierophants, prelates, obeah-men, abbés, nuns, missionaries, exhorters, deacons, friars, hadjis, high-priests, muezzins, brahmins, medicine-men, confessors, eminences, elders, primates, prebendaries, pilgrims, prophets, imaums, beneficiaries, clerks, vicars-choral, archbishops, bishops, abbots, priors, preachers, padres, abbotesses, caloyers, palmers, curates, patriarchs, bonezs, santons, beadsmen, canonesses, residentiaries, diocesans, deans, subdeans, rural deans, abdals, charm-sellers, archdeacons, hierarchs, class-leaders, incumbents, capitulars, sheiks, talapoins, postulants, scribes, gooroos, precentors, beadles, fakeers, sextons, reverences, revivalists, cenobites, perpetual curates, chaplains, mudjoes, readers, novices, vicars, pastors, rabbis, ulemas, lamas, sacristans, vergers, dervises, lectors, church wardens, cardinals, prioresses, suffragans, acolytes, rectors, cures, sophis, mutifs and pumpums.

Influence, *n.* In politics, a visionary *quo* given in exchange for a substantial *quid.*

Ingrate, *n.* One who receives a benefit from another, or is otherwise an object of charity.

Injury, *n.* An offense next in degree of enormity to a slight.

Injustice, *n.* A burden which of all those that we load upon others and carry ourselves is lightest in the hands and heaviest upon the back.

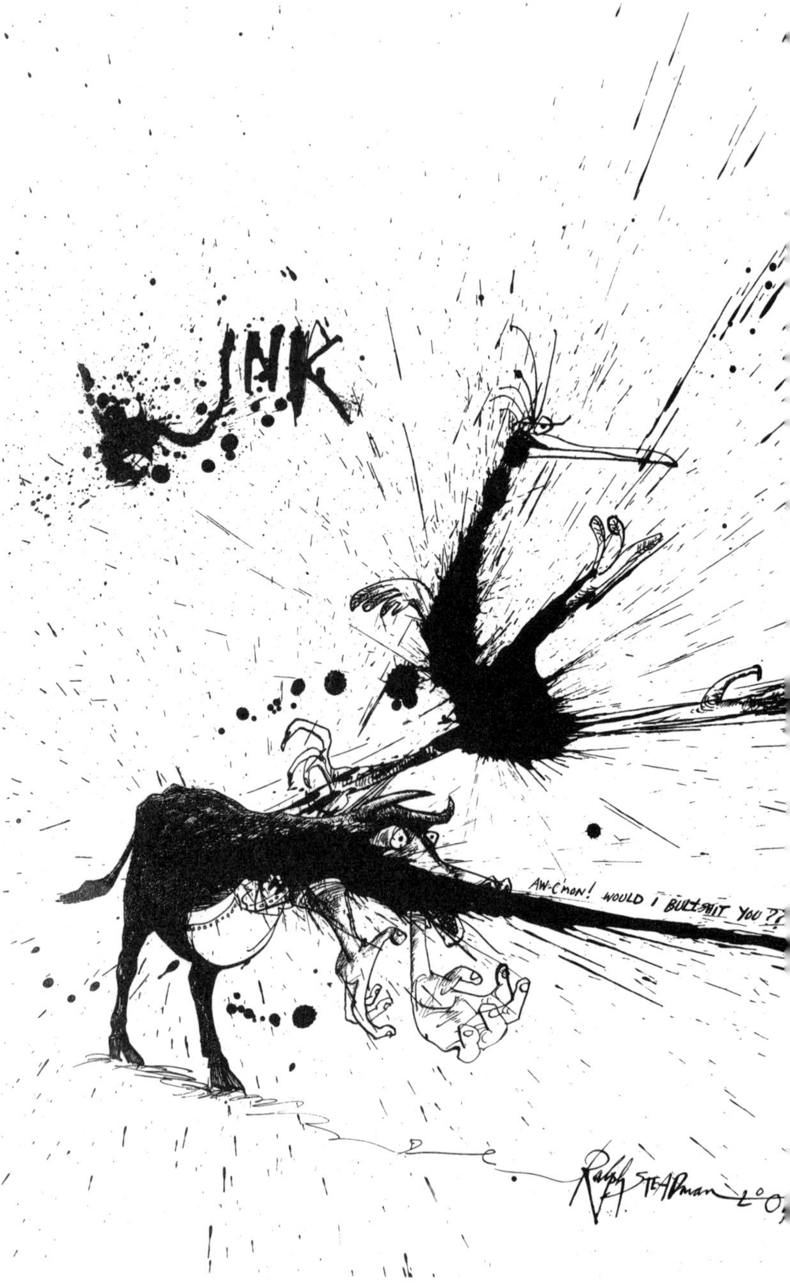
INK
AW-C'MON! WOULD I BULLSHIT YOU??
Ralph STEADman

Ink, *n.* A villainous compound of tanno-gallate of iron, gum-arabic and water, chiefly used to facilitate the infection of idiocy and promote intellectual crime. The properties of ink are peculiar and contradictory: it may be used to make reputations and unmake them; to blacken them and to make them white; but it is most generally and acceptably employed as a mortar to bind together the stones in an edifice of fame, and as a whitewash to conceal afterward the rascal quality of the material. There are men called journalists who have established ink baths which some persons pay money to get into, others to get out of. Not infrequently it occurs that a person who has paid to get in pays twice as much to get out.

Innate, *adj.* Natural, inherent – as innate ideas, that is to say, ideas that we are born with, having had them previously imparted to us. The doctrine of innate ideas is one of the most admirable faiths of philosophy, being itself an innate idea and therefore inaccessible to disproof, though Locke foolishly supposed himself to have given it 'a black eye.' Among innate ideas may be mentioned the belief in one's ability to conduct a newspaper, in the greatness of one's country, in the superiority of one's civilization, in the importance of one's personal affairs, and in the interesting nature of one's diseases.

Insurance, *n.* An ingenious modern game of chance in which the player is permitted to enjoy the comfortable conviction that he is beating the man who keeps the table.

INSURANCE AGENT: My dear sir, that is a fine house – pray let me insure it.

HOUSE OWNER: With pleasure. Please make the annual premium so low that by the time when, according to the tables of your actuary, it will probably be destroyed by fire I will have paid you considerably less than the face of the policy.

INSURANCE AGENT: O dear, no – we could not afford to do that. We must fix the premium so that you will have paid more.

HOUSE OWNER: How, then, can *I* afford *that*?

INSURANCE AGENT: Why, your house may burn down at any time. There was Smith's house, for example, which –

HOUSE OWNER: Spare me – there were Brown's house, on the contrary, and Jones's house, and Robinson's house, which –

INSURANCE AGENT: Spare *me*!

HOUSE OWNER: Let us understand each other. You want me to pay you money on the supposition that something will occur previously to the time set by yourself for its occurrence. In other words, you expect me to bet that my house will not last so long as you say that it will probably last.

INSURANCE AGENT: But if your house burns without insurance it will be a total loss.

HOUSE OWNER: Beg your pardon – by your own actuary's tables I shall probably have saved, when it burns, all the premiums I would otherwise have paid to you – amounting to more than the face of the policy they would have bought. But suppose it to burn, uninsured, before the time upon which your figures are based. If

I could not afford that, how could you if it were insured?

INSURANCE AGENT: O, we should make ourselves whole from our luckier ventures with other clients. Virtually, they pay your loss.

HOUSE OWNER: And virtually, then, don't I help to pay their losses? Are not their houses as likely as mine to burn before they have paid you as much as you must pay them? The case stands this way: you expect to take more money from your clients than you pay to them, do you not?

INSURANCE AGENT: Certainly; if we did not —

HOUSE OWNER: I would not trust you with my money. Very well, then. If it is *certain*, with reference to the whole body of your clients, that they lose money on you it is *probable*, with reference to any one of them, that *he* will. It is these individual probabilities that made the aggregate certainty.

INSURANCE AGENT: I will not deny it — but look at the figures in this pamph —

HOUSE OWNER: Heaven forbid!

INSURANCE AGENT: You spoke of saving the premiums which you would otherwise pay to me. Will you not be more likely to squander them? We offer you an incentive to thrift.

HOUSE OWNER: The willingness of A to take care of B's money is not peculiar to insurance, but as a charitable institution you command esteem. Deign to accept its expression from a Deserving Object.

65

Insurrection, *n.* An unsuccessful revolution. Disaffection's failure to substitute misrule for bad government.

Intention, *n.* The mind's sense of the prevalence of one set of influences over another set; an effect whose cause is the imminence, immediate or remote, of the performance of an involuntary act.

Interpreter, *n.* One who enables two persons of different languages to understand each other by repeating to each what it would have been to the interpreter's advantage for the other to have said.

Interregnum, *n.* The period during which a monarchical country is governed by a warm spot on the cushion of a throne. The experiment of letting the spot grow cold has commonly been attended by most unhappy results from the zeal of many worthy persons to make it warm again.

Intimacy, *n.* A relation into which fools are providentially drawn for their mutual destruction.

Introduction, *n.* A social ceremony invented by the devil for the gratification of his servants and the plaguing of his enemies. The introduction attains its most malevolent development in this country, being, indeed, closely related to our political system. Every American being the equal of every other American, it follows that everybody has the right to know everybody else, which implies the right to introduce without request or permission. The Declaration of Independence should have read thus:

'We hold these truths to be self-evident: that all men are created equal; that they are endowed by their Creator with certain inalienable rights; that among these are life, and the right to make that of another miserable by thrusting upon him an incalculable quantity of acquaintances; liberty, particularly the liberty to introduce persons to one another without first ascertaining if they are not already acquainted as enemies; and the pursuit of another's happiness with a running pack of strangers.'

Inventor, *n.* A person who makes an ingenious arrangement of wheels, levers and springs, and believes it civilization.

Irreligion, *n.* The principal one of the great faiths of the world.

J is a consonant in English, but some nations use it as a vowel – than which nothing could be more absurd. Its original form, which has been but slightly modified, was that of the tail of a subdued dog, and it was not a letter but a character, standing for a Latin verb, *jacere*, 'to throw,' because when a stone is thrown at a dog the dog's tail assumes that shape. This is the origin of the letter, as expounded by the renowned Dr Jocolpus Bumer, of the University of Belgrade, who established his conclusions on the subject in a work of three quarto volumes and committed suicide on being reminded that the j in the Roman alphabet had originally no curl.

Jealous, *adj.* Unduly concerned about the preservation of that which can be lost only if not worth keeping.

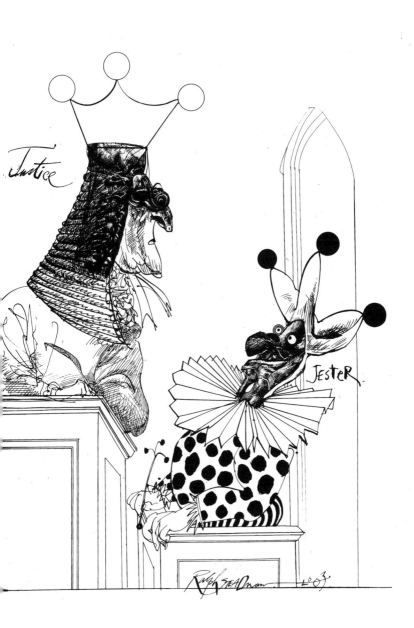

Jester, *n.* An officer formerly attached to a king's household, whose business it was to amuse the court by ludicrous actions and utterances, the absurdity being attested by his motley costume. The king himself being attired with dignity, it took the world some centuries to discover that his own conduct and decrees were sufficiently ridiculous for the amusement not only of his court but of all mankind.

Justice, *n.* A commodity which in a more or less adulterated condition the State sells to the citizen as a reward for his allegiance, taxes and personal service.

Kill, *v.t.* To create a vacancy without nominating a successor.

Kilt, *n.* A costume sometimes worn by Scotchmen in America and Americans in Scotland.

Kindness, *n.* A brief preface to ten volumes of exaction.

King, *n.* A male person commonly known in America as a 'crowned head,' although he never wears a crown and has usually no head to speak of.

Kiss, *n.* A word invented by the poets as a rhyme for 'bliss.' It is supposed to signify, in a general way, some kind of rite or ceremony appertaining to a good understanding;

but the manner of its performance is unknown to this lexicographer.

Kleptomaniac, *n.* A rich thief.

Labor, *n.* One of the processes by which A acquires property for B.

Land, *n.* A part of the earth's surface, considered as property. The theory that land is property subject to private ownership and control is the foundation of modern society, and is eminently worthy of the superstructure. Carried to its logical conclusion, it means that some have the right to prevent others from living; for the right to own implies the right exclusively to occupy; and in fact laws of trespass are enacted wherever property in land is recognized. It follows that if the whole area of *terra firma* is owned by A, B and C, there will be no place for D, E, F and G to be born, or, born as trespassers, to exist.

Language, *n.* The music with which we charm the serpents guarding another's treasure.

Lap, *n.* One of the most important organs of the female system – an admirable provision of nature for the repose of infancy, but chiefly useful in rural festivities to support plates of cold chicken and heads of adult males. The male of our species has a rudimentary lap, imperfectly developed and in no way contributing to the animal's substantial welfare.

Laughter, *n.* An interior convulsion, producing a distortion of the features and accompanied by inarticulate noises. It is infectious and, though intermittent, incurable.

Laureate, *adj.* Crowned with leaves of the laurel. In England the Poet Laureate is an officer of the sovereign's court, acting as dancing skeleton at every royal feast and singing-mute at every royal funeral.

Laurel, *n.* The *laurus*, a vegetable dedicated to Apollo, and formerly defoliated to wreathe the brows of victors and such poets as had influence at court. (*Vide Supra.*)

Lawful, *adj.* Compatible with the will of a judge having jurisdiction.

Lawyer, *n.* One skilled in circumvention of the law.

Laziness, *n.* Unwarranted repose of manner in a person of low degree.

Lead, *n.* A heavy blue-gray metal much used in giving stability to light lovers – particularly to those who love

not wisely but other men's wives. Lead is also of great service as a counterpoise to an argument of such weight that it turns the scale of debate the wrong way. An interesting fact in the chemistry of international controversy is that at the point of contact of two patriotisms lead is precipitated in great quantities.

Learning, *n.* The kind of ignorance distinguishing the studious.

Lecturer, *n.* One with his hand in your pocket, his tongue in your ear and his faith in your patience.

Legacy, *n.* A gift from one who is legging it out of this vale of tears.

Lexicographer, *n.* A pestilent fellow who, under the pretense of recording some particular stage in the development of a language, does what he can to arrest its growth, stiffen its flexibility and mechanize its methods. For your lexicographer, having written his dictionary, comes to be considered 'as one having authority,' whereas his function is only to make a record, not to give a law. The natural servility of the human understanding having invested him with judicial power, surrenders its right of reason and submits itself to a chronicle as if it were a statute. Let the dictionary (for example) mark a good word as 'obsolete' or 'obsolescent' and few men thereafter venture to use it, whatever their need of it and however desirable its restoration to favor – whereby the process of impoverishment is accelerated and speech decays. On the contrary, the bold and discerning writer who, recognizing the truth that language must grow by innovation if it grow at all, makes new words and uses the old in an unfamiliar sense, has no following and is tartly reminded that 'it isn't in the dictionary' – although down to the time of the first lexicographer (Heaven forgive him!) no author ever had used a word that *was* in the dictionary. In the golden prime and high noon of English speech; when from the lips of the great Elizabethans fell words that made their own meaning and carried it in their very sound; when a Shakespeare and a Bacon were possible, and the language now rapidly perishing at one end and slowly renewed at the other was in vigorous growth and hardy preservation – sweeter than honey and stronger than a lion – the lexicographer was a person unknown, the dictionary a creation which his Creator had not created him to create.

Liar, *n.* A lawyer with a roving commission.

Liberty, *n.* One of Imagination's most precious possessions.

Lickspittle, *n.* A useful functionary, not infrequently found editing a newspaper. In his character of editor he is closely allied to the blackmailer by the tie of occasional identity; for in truth the lickspittle is only the blackmailer under another aspect, though the latter is frequently found as an independent species. Lickspittling is more detestable than blackmailing, precisely as the business of a confidence man is more detestable than that of a highway robber; and the parallel maintains itself throughout, for whereas few robbers will cheat, every sneak will plunder if he dare.

Life, *n.* A spiritual pickle preserving the body from decay. We live in daily apprehension of its loss; yet when lost it is not missed. The question, 'Is life worth living?' has been much discussed; particularly by those who think it is not, many of whom have written at great length in support of their view and by careful observance of the laws of health enjoyed for long terms of years the honors of successful controversy.

Lighthouse, *n.* A tall building on the seashore in which the government maintains a lamp and the friend of a politician.

Litigant, *n.* A person about to give up his skin for the hope of retaining his bones.

Litigation, *n.* A machine which you go into as a pig and come out of as a sausage.

Liver, *n.* A large red organ thoughtfully provided by nature to be bilious with. The sentiments and emotions which every literary anatomist now knows to haunt the heart were anciently believed to infest the liver.

LL.D. Letters indicating the degree *Legumptionorum Doctor*, one learned in laws, gifted with legal gumption. Some suspicion is cast upon this derivation by the fact that the title was formerly *£.£.d.*, and conferred only upon gentlemen distinguished for their wealth. At the date of this writing Columbia University is considering the expediency of making another degree for clergymen, in place of the old D.D. – *Damnator Diaboli*. The new honor will be known as *Sanctorum Custus*, and written *$$c*.

Lock-and-key, *n.* The distinguishing device of civilization and enlightenment.

Logic, *n.* The art of thinking and reasoning in strict accordance with the limitations and incapacities of the human misunderstanding. The basic of logic is the syllogism, consisting of a major and a minor premise and a conclusion – thus:

Major Premise: Sixty men can do a piece of work sixty times as quickly as one man.

Minor Premise: One man can dig a post-hole in sixty seconds; therefore – *Conclusion*: Sixty men can dig a post-hole in one second.

This may be called the syllogism arithmetical, in which, by combining logic and mathematics, we obtain a double certainty and are twice blessed.

Logomachy, *n.* A war in which the weapons are words and the wounds punctures in the swim-bladder of self-esteem – a kind of contest in which, the vanquished being unconscious of defeat, the victor is denied the reward of success.

Longanimity, *n.* The disposition to endure injury with meek forbearance while maturing a plan of revenge.

Longevity, *n.* Uncommon extension of the fear of death.

Looking-glass, *n.* A vitreous plane upon which to display a fleeting show for man's disillusion given.

The King of Manchuria had a magic looking-glass, whereon whoso looked saw, not his own image, but only that of the king. A certain courtier who had long enjoyed the king's favor and was thereby enriched beyond any other subject of the realm, said to the king: 'Give me, I pray, thy wonderful mirror, so that when absent out of thine august presence I may yet do homage before thy visible shadow, prostrating myself night and morning in the glory of thy benign countenance, as which nothing has so divine splendor, O Noonday Sun of the Universe!'

Pleased with the speech, the king commanded that the mirror be conveyed to the courtier's palace; but after, having gone thither without apprisal, he found it in an apartment where was naught but idle lumber. And the mirror was dimmed with dust and overlaced with cobwebs. This so angered him that he fisted it hard, shattering the glass, and was sorely hurt. Enraged all the more by this mischance, he commanded that the ungrateful courtier be thrown into prison, and that the glass be repaired and taken back to his own palace; and this was done. But when the king looked again on the mirror he saw not his image as before, but only the figure of a crowned ass, having a bloody bandage on one of its hinder hooves – as the artificers and all who had looked upon it had before discerned but feared to report. Taught wisdom and charity, the king restored his courtier to liberty, had the mirror set into the back of the throne and reigned many years with justice and humility; and one day when he fell asleep in death while on the throne, the whole court saw in the mirror the luminous figure of an angel, which remains to this day.

Loquacity, *n.* A disorder which renders the sufferer unable to curb his tongue when you wish to talk.

Lore, *n.* Learning – particularly that sort which is not derived from a regular course of instruction but comes of the reading of occult books, or by nature. This latter is commonly designated as folklore and embraces popularly myths and superstitions. In Baring-Gould's *Curious Myths of the Middle Ages* the reader will find many of these traced backward, through various peoples on converging lines, toward a common origin in remote antiquity. Among these are the fables of 'Teddy the Giant Killer,' 'The Sleeping John Sharp Williams,' 'Little Red Riding Hood and the Sugar Trust,' 'Beauty and the Brisbane,' 'The Seven Aldermen of Ephesus,' 'Rip Van Fairbanks,' and so forth. The fable which Goethe so affectingly relates under the title of 'The Erl-King' was known two thousand years ago in Greece as 'The Demos and the Infant Industry.' One of the most general and ancient of these myths is that Arabian tale of 'Ali Baba and the Forty Rockefellers.'

Loss, *n.* Privation of that which we had, or had not. Thus, in the latter sense, it is said of a defeated candidate that he 'lost his election'; and of that eminent man, the poet Gilder, that he has 'lost his mind.'

Love, *n.* A temporary insanity curable by marriage or by removal of the patient from the influences under which he incurred the disorder. This disease, like *caries* and many other ailments, is prevalent only among civilized races living under artificial conditions; barbarous nations breathing pure air and eating simple food enjoy immunity from its ravages. It is sometimes fatal, but more frequently to the physician than to the patient.

Low-bred, *adj.* 'Raised' instead of brought up.

Luminary, *n.* One who throws light upon a subject; as an editor by not writing about it.

Lunarian, *n.* An inhabitant of the moon, as distinguished from Lunatic, one whom the moon inhabits. The Lunarians have been described by Lucian, Locke and other observers, but without much agreement. For example, Bragellos avers their anatomical identity with Man, but Professor Newcomb says they are more like the hill tribes of Vermont.

Lyre, *n.* An ancient instrument of torture.

Mace, *n.* A staff of office signifying authority. Its form, that of a heavy club, indicates its original purpose and use in dissuading from dissent.

Machination, *n.* The method employed by one's opponents in baffling one's open and honorable efforts to do the right thing.

Mad, *adj.* Affected with a high degree of intellectual independence; not conforming to standards of thought, speech and action derived by the conformants from study of themselves; at odds with the majority; in short, unusual. It is noteworthy that persons are pronounced mad by officials destitute of evidence that themselves are sane. For illustration, this present (and illustrious) lexicographer is

84

no firmer in the faith of his own sanity than is any inmate of any madhouse in the land; yet for aught he knows to the contrary, instead of the lofty occupation that seems to him to be engaging his powers he may really be beating his hands against the window bars of an asylum and declaring himself Noah Webster, to the innocent delight of many thoughtless spectators.

Magic, *n.* An art of converting superstition into coin. There are other arts serving the same high purpose, but the discreet lexicographer does not name them.

Magnet, *n.* Something acted upon by magnetism.

Magnetism, *n.* Something acting upon a magnet.

The two definitions immediately foregoing are condensed from the works of one thousand eminent scientists, who have illuminated the subject with a great white light, to the inexpressible advancement of human knowledge.

Magnificent, *adj.* Having a grandeur or splendor superior to that to which the spectator is accustomed, as the ears of an ass, to a rabbit, or the glory of a glow-worm, to a maggot.

Magnitude, *n.* Size. Magnitude being purely relative, nothing is large and nothing small. If everything in the universe were increased in bulk one thousand diameters nothing would be any larger than it was before, but if one thing remained unchanged all the others would be larger than they had been. To an understanding familiar with the relativity of magnitude and distance the spaces and masses of the astronomer would be no more impressive than those of the microscopist. For anything we know to the contrary, the visible universe may be a small part of an atom, with its component ions, floating in the life-fluid (luminiferous ether) of some animal. Possibly the wee creatures peopling the corpuscles of our own blood are overcome with the proper emotion when contemplating the unthinkable distance from one of these to another.

Magpie, *n.* A bird whose thievish disposition suggested to some one that it might be taught to talk.

Maiden, *n.* A young person of the unfair sex addicted to clewless conduct and views that madden to crime. The genus has a wide geographical distribution, being found wherever sought and deplored wherever found. The maiden is not altogether unpleasing to the eye, nor (without her piano and her views) insupportable to the ear, though in respect to comeliness distinctly inferior to the rainbow, and, with regard to the part of her that is audible, beaten out of the field by the canary – which, also, is more portable.

Majesty, *n.* The state and title of a king. Regarded with a just contempt by the Most Eminent Grand Masters, Grand Chancellors, Great Incohonees and Imperial Potentates of the ancient and honorable orders of republican America.

Male, *n.* A member of the unconsidered, or negligible sex. The male of the human race is commonly known

(to the female) as Mere Man. The genus has two varieties: good providers and bad providers.

Malefactor, *n.* The chief factor in the progress of the human race.

Malthusian, *adj.* Pertaining to Malthus and his doctrines. Malthus believed in artificially limiting population, but found that it could not be done by talking. One of the most practical exponents of the Malthusian idea was Herod of Judea, though all the famous soldiers have been of the same way of thinking.

Mammalia, *n. pl.* A family of vertebrate animals whose females in a state of nature suckle their young, but when civilized and enlightened put them out to nurse, or use the bottle.

Mammon, *n.* The god of the world's leading religion. His chief temple is in the holy city of New York.

Man, *n.* An animal so lost in rapturous contemplation of what he thinks he is as to overlook what he indubitably ought to be. His chief occupation is extermination of other animals and his own species, which, however, multiplies with such insistent rapidity as to infest the whole habitable earth and Canada.

Manicheism, *n.* The ancient Persian doctrine of an incessant warfare between Good and Evil. When Good gave up the fight the Persians joined the victorious Opposition.

Manna, *n.* A food miraculously given to the Israelites in the wilderness. When it was no longer supplied to them they settled down and tilled the soil, fertilizing it, as a rule, with the bodies of the original occupants.

Marriage, *n.* The state or condition of a community consisting of a master, a mistress and two slaves, making in all, two.

Martyr, *n.* One who moves along the line of least reluctance to a desired death.

Material, *adj.* Having an actual existence, as distinguished from an imaginary one. Important.

Mausoleum, *n.* The final and funniest folly of the rich.

Mayonnaise, *n.* One of the sauces which serve the French in place of a state religion.

Me, *pro.* The objectionable case of I. The personal pronoun in English has three cases, the dominative, the objectionable and the oppressive. Each is all three.

Meander, *n.* To proceed sinuously and aimlessly. The word is the ancient name of a river about one hundred and fifty miles south of Troy, which turned and twisted in the effort to get out of hearing when the Greeks and Trojans boasted of their prowess.

Medal, *n.* A small metal disk given as a reward for virtues, attainments or services more or less authentic.

It is related of Bismarck, who had been awarded a medal for gallantly rescuing a drowning person, that, being asked the meaning of the medal, he replied: 'I save lives some-times.' And sometimes he didn't.

Medicine, *n.* A stone flung down the Bowery to kill a dog in Broadway.

Meekness, *n.* Uncommon patience in planning a revenge that is worth while.

Mendacious, *adj.* Addicted to rhetoric.

Merchant, *n.* One engaged in a commercial pursuit. A commercial pursuit is one in which the thing pursued is a dollar.

Mercy, *n.* An attribute beloved of detected offenders.

Mesmerism, *n.* Hypnotism before it wore good clothes, kept a carriage and asked Incredulity to dinner.

Metropolis, *n.* A stronghold of provincialism.

Millennium, *n.* The period of a thousand years when the lid is to be screwed down, with all reformers on the under side.

Mind, *n.* A mysterious form of matter secreted by the brain. Its chief activity consists in the endeavor to ascertain its own nature, the futility of the attempt being due to the fact that it has nothing but itself to know itself with.

Mine, *adj.* Belonging to me if I can hold or seize it.

Minister, *n.* An agent of a higher power with a lower

responsibility. In diplomacy an officer sent into a foreign country as the visible embodiment of his sovereign's hostility. His principal qualification is a degree of plausible inveracity next below that of an ambassador.

Minor, *adj.* Less objectionable.

Miracle, *n.* An act or event out of the order of nature and unaccountable, as beating a normal hand of four kings and an ace with four aces and a king.

Miscreant, *n.* A person of the highest degree of unworth. Etymologically, the word means unbeliever, and its present signification may be regarded as theology's noblest contribution to the development of our language.

Misdemeanor, *n.* An infraction of the law having less dignity than a felony and constituting no claim to admittance into the best criminal society.

Misericorde, *n.* A dagger which in mediæval warfare was used by the foot soldier to remind an unhorsed knight that he was mortal.

Misfortune, *n.* The kind of fortune that never misses.

Miss, *n.* A title with which we brand unmarried women to indicate that they are in the market. Miss, Missis (Mrs) and Mister (Mr) are the three most distinctly disagreeable words in the language, in sound and sense. Two are corruptions of Mistress, the other of Master. In the general abolition of social titles in this our country they miraculously escaped to plague us. If we must have them let us be consistent and give one to the unmarried man. I venture to suggest Mush, abbreviated to Mh.

Molecule, *n.* The ultimate, indivisible unit of matter. It is distinguished from the corpuscle, also the ultimate, indivisible unit of matter, by a closer resemblance to the atom, also the ultimate, indivisible unit of matter. Three great scientific theories of the structure of the universe are the molecular, the corpuscular and the atomic. A fourth affirms, with Haeckel, the condensation or precipitation of matter from ether – whose existence is proved by the condensation or precipitation. The present trend of scientific thought is toward the theory of ions. The ion differs from the molecule, the corpuscle and the atom in that it is an ion. A fifth theory is held by idiots, but it is doubtful if they know any more about the matter than the others.

Monarch, *n.* A person engaged in reigning. Formerly the monarch ruled, as the derivation of the word attests, and as many subjects have had occasion to learn. In Russia and the Orient the monarch has still a considerable influence in public affairs and in the disposition of the human head, but in Western Europe political administration is mostly entrusted to his ministers, he being somewhat preoccupied with reflections relating to the status of his own head.

Monarchical Government, *n.* Government.

Monday, *n.* In Christian countries, the day after the baseball game.

Money, *n.* A blessing that is of no advantage to us excepting when we part with it. An evidence of culture and a passport to polite society. Supportable property.

Monkey, *n.* An arboreal animal which makes itself at home in genealogical trees.

Monsignor, *n.* A high ecclesiastical title, of which the Founder of our religion overlooked the advantages.

Monument, *n.* A structure intended to commemorate something which either needs no commemoration or cannot be commemorated.

Moral, *adj.* Conforming to a local and mutable standard of right. Having the quality of general expediency.

More, *adj.* The comparative degree of too much.

Mouse, *n.* An animal which strews its path with fainting women. As in Rome Christians were thrown to the lions, so centuries earlier in Otumwee, the most ancient and famous city of the world, female heretics were thrown to the mice.

Mousquetaire, *n.* A long glove covering a part of the arm. Worn in New Jersey. But 'mousquetaire' is a mighty poor way to spell muskeeter.

Mouth, *n.* In man, the gateway to the soul; in woman, the outlet of the heart.

Mugwump, *n.* In politics one afflicted with self-respect and addicted to the vice of independence. A term of contempt.

Mulatto, *n.* A child of two races, ashamed of both.

Multitude, *n.* A crowd; the source of political wisdom and virtue. In a republic, the object of the statesman's adoration. A multitude is as wise as its wisest member if it obey him; if not, it is no wiser than its most foolish.

Mummy, *n.* An ancient Egyptian, formerly in universal use among modern civilized nations as medicine, and now engaged in supplying art with an excellent pigment. He is handy, too, in museums in gratifying the vulgar curiosity that serves to distinguish man from the lower animals.

Mustang, *n.* An indocile horse of the western plains. In English society the American wife of an English nobleman.

Mythology, *n.* The body of a primitive people's beliefs concerning its origin, early history, heroes, deities and so forth, as distinguished from the true accounts which it invents later.

Nectar, *n.* A drink served at banquets of the Olympian deities. The secret of its preparation is lost, but the modern Kentuckians believe that they come pretty near to a knowledge of its chief ingredient.

Neighbor, *n.* One whom we are commanded to love as ourselves, and who does all he knows how to make us disobedient.

Nepotism, *n.* Appointing your grandmother to office for the good of the party.

Newtonian, *adj.* Pertaining to a philosophy of the universe, invented by Newton, who discovered that an apple will fall to the ground, but was unable to say why. His successors and disciples have advanced so far as to be able to say when.

Nirvana, *n.* In the Buddhist religion, a state of pleasurable annihilation awarded to the wise, particularly to those wise enough to understand it.

Nobleman, *n.* Nature's provision for wealthy American maids ambitious to incur social distinction and suffer high life.

Noise, *n.* A stench in the ear. Undomesticated music. The chief product and authenticating sign of civilization.

Nominee, *n.* A modest gentleman shrinking from the distinction of private life and diligently seeking the honorable obscurity of public office.

Non-combatant, *n.* A dead Quaker.

Nonsense, *n.* The objections that are urged against this excellent dictionary.

Nose, *n.* The extreme outpost of the face. From the circumstance that great conquerors have great noses, Getius, whose writings antedate the age of humor, calls the nose the organ of quell. It has been observed that one's nose is never so happy as when thrust into the affairs of another, from which some physiologists have drawn the inference that the nose is devoid of the sense of smell.

Notoriety, *n.* The fame of one's competitor for public honors. The kind of renown most accessible and acceptable to mediocrity.

Noumenon, *n.* That which exists, as distinguished from that which merely seems to exist, the latter being a phenomenon. The noumenon is a bit difficult to locate; it can be apprehended only by a process of reasoning – which is a phenomenon. Nevertheless, the discovery and exposition of noumena offer a rich field for what Lewes calls 'the endless variety and excitement of philosophic thought.' Hurrah (therefore) for the noumenon!

Novel, *n.* A short story padded. A species of composition bearing the same relation to literature that the panorama bears to art. As it is too long to be read at a sitting the impressions made by its successive parts are successively effaced, as in the panorama. Unity, totality of effect, is impossible; for besides the few pages last read all that is carried in mind is the mere plot of what has gone before. To the romance the novel is what photography is to painting. Its distinguishing principle, probability, corresponds to the literal actuality of the photograph and puts it distinctly into the category of reporting; whereas the free wing of the romancer enables him to mount to such altitudes of imagination as he may be fitted to attain; and the first three essentials of the literary art are imagination, imagination and imagination. The art of writing novels, such as it was, is long dead everywhere except in Russia, where it is new. Peace to its ashes – some of which have a large sale.

November, *n.* The eleventh twelfth of a weariness.

Oath, *n.* In law, a solemn appeal to the Deity, made binding upon the conscience by a penalty for perjury.

Oblivion, *n.* The state or condition in which the wicked cease from struggling and the dreary are at rest. Fame's eternal dumping ground. Cold storage for high hopes. A place where ambitious authors meet their works without pride and their betters without envy. A dormitory without an alarm clock.

Observatory, *n.* A place where astronomers conjecture away the guesses of their predecessors.

Obsolete, *adj.* No longer used by the timid. Said chiefly of words. A word which some lexicographer has marked

obsolete is ever thereafter an object of dread and loathing to the fool writer, but if it is a good word and has no exact modern equivalent equally good, it is good enough for the good writer. Indeed, a writer's attitude toward 'obsolete' words is as true a measure of his literary ability as anything except the character of his work. A dictionary of obsolete and obsolescent words would not only be singularly rich in strong and sweet parts of speech; it would add large possessions to the vocabulary of every competent writer who might not happen to be a competent reader.

Obstinate, *adj.* Inaccessible to the truth as it is manifest in the splendor and stress of our advocacy.

Occasional, *adj.* Afflicting us with greater or less frequency. That, however, is not the sense in which the word is used in the phrase 'occasional verses,' which are verses written for an 'occasion,' such as an anniversary, a celebration or other event. True, they afflict us a little worse than other sorts of verse, but their name has no reference to irregular recurrence.

Occident, *n.* The part of the world lying west (or east) of the Orient. It is largely inhabited by Christians, a powerful sub-tribe of the Hypocrites, whose principal industries are murder and cheating, which they are pleased to call 'war' and 'commerce.' These, also, are the principal industries of the Orient.

Ocean, *n.* A body of water occupying about two-thirds of a world made for man – who has no gills.

Offensive, *adj.* Generating disagreeable emotions or sensations, as the advance of an army against its enemy.

Old, *adj.* In that stage of usefulness which is not inconsistent with general inefficiency, as an *old man.* Discredited by lapse of time and offensive to the popular taste, as an *old* book.

Oleaginous, *adj.* Oily, smooth, sleek.

Disraeli once described the manner of Bishop Wilberforce as 'unctuous, oleaginous, saponaceous.' And the good prelate was ever afterward known as Soapy Sam. For every man there is something in the vocabulary that would stick to him like a second skin. His enemies have only to find it.

Olympian, *adj.* Relating to a mountain in Thessaly, once inhabited by gods, now a repository of yellowing newspapers, beer bottles and mutilated sardine cans, attesting the presence of the tourist and his appetite.

Omen, *n.* A sign that something will happen if nothing happens.

Once, *adv.* Enough.

Opera, *n.* A play representing life in another world, whose inhabitants have no speech but song, no motions but gestures and no postures but attitudes. All acting is simulation, and the word *simulation* is from *simia*, an ape; but in opera the actor takes for his model *Simia audibilis* (or *Pithecanthropos stentor*) – the ape that howls.

Opiate, *n.* An unlocked door in the prison of Identity. It leads into the jail yard.

Opportunity, *n.* A favorable occasion for grasping a disappointment.

Oppose, *v.* To assist with obstructions and objections.

Opposition, *n.* In politics the party that prevents the Government from running amuck by hamstringing it.

Optimism, *n.* The doctrine, or belief that everything is beautiful, including what is ugly, everything good, especially the bad, and everything right that is wrong. It is held with greatest tenacity by those most accustomed to the mischance of falling into adversity, and is most acceptably expounded with the grin that apes a smile. Being a blind faith, it is inaccessible to the light of disproof – an intellectual disorder, yielding to no treatment but death. It is hereditary, but fortunately not contagious.

Optimist, *n.* A proponent of the doctrine that black is white.

Oratory, *n.* A conspiracy between speech and action to cheat the understanding. A tyranny tempered by stenography.

Orphan, *n.* A living person whom death has deprived of the power of filial ingratitude – a privation appealing with a particular eloquence to all that is sympathetic in human nature. When young the orphan is commonly sent to an asylum, where by careful cultivation of its rudimentary sense of locality it is taught to know its place. It is then instructed in the arts of dependence and servitude and eventually turned loose to prey upon the world as a boot-black or scullery maid.

Orthodox, *n.* An ox wearing the popular religious yoke.

Orthography, *n.* The science of spelling by the eye instead of the ear. Advocated with more heat than light by the outmates of every asylum for the insane. They have had to concede a few things since the time of Chaucer, but are none the less hot in defence of those to be conceded hereafter.

Otherwise, *adv.* No better.

Outcome, *n.* A particular type of disappointment. By the kind of intelligence that sees in an exception a proof of the rule the wisdom of an act is judged by the outcome, the result. This is immortal nonsense; the wisdom of an act is to be judged by the light that the doer had when he performed it.

Outdo, *v.t.* To make an enemy.

Out-of-doors, *n.* That part of one's environment upon which no government has been able to collect taxes. Chiefly useful to inspire poets.

Ovation, *n.* In ancient Rome, a definite, formal pageant in honor of one who had been disserviceable to the enemies of the nation. A lesser 'triumph.' In modern English the word is improperly used to signify any loose and spontaneous expression of popular homage to the hero of the hour and place.

Overeat, *v.* To dine.

Overwork, *n.* A dangerous disorder affecting high public functionaries who want to go fishing.

Owe, *v.* To have (and to hold) a debt. The word formerly signified not indebtedness, but possession; meant 'own,' and in the minds of debtors there is still a good deal of confusion between assets and liabilities.

Oyster, *n.* A slimy, gobby shellfish which civilization gives men the hardihood to eat without removing its entrails! The shells are sometimes given to the poor.

Pain, *n.* An uncomfortable frame of mind that may have a physical basis in something that is being done to the body, or may be purely mental, caused by the good fortune of another.

Painting, *n.* The art of protecting flat surfaces from the weather and exposing them to the critic.

Formerly, painting and sculpture were combined in the same work: the ancients painted their statues. The only present alliance between the two arts is that the modern painter chisels his patrons.

Palace, *n.* A fine and costly residence, particularly that of a great official. The residence of a high dignitary of the Christian Church is called a palace; that of the Founder of his religion was known as a field, or wayside. There is progress.

Palm, *n.* A species of tree having several varieties, of which the familiar 'itching palm' (*Palma hominis*) is most widely distributed and sedulously cultivated. This noble vegetable exudes a kind of invisible gum, which may be detected by applying to the bark a piece of gold or silver. The metal will adhere with remarkable tenacity. The fruit of the itching palm is so bitter and unsatisfying that a considerable percentage of it is sometimes given away in what are known as 'benefactions.'

Palmistry, *n.* The 947th method (according to Mimbleshaw's classification) of obtaining money by false pretences. It consists in 'reading character' in the wrinkles made by closing the hand. The pretence is not altogether false; character can really be read very accurately in this way, for the wrinkles in every hand submitted plainly spell the word 'dupe.' The imposture consists in not reading it aloud.

Pandemonium, *n.* Literally, the Place of All the Demons. Most of them have escaped into politics and finance, and the place is now used as a lecture hall by the Audible Reformer. When disturbed by his voice the ancient echoes clamor appropriate responses most gratifying to his pride of distinction.

Pantaloons, *n.* A nether habiliment of the adult civilized male. The garment is tubular and unprovided with hinges at the points of flexion. Supposed to have been invented by a humorist. Called 'trousers' by the enlightened and 'pants' by the unworthy.

Pantheism, *n.* The doctrine that everything is God, in contradistinction to the doctrine that God is everything.

Pantomime, *n.* A play in which the story is told without violence to the language. The least disagreeable form of dramatic action.

Pardon, *v.* To remit a penalty and restore to a life of crime. To add to the lure of crime the temptation of ingratitude.

Passport, *n.* A document treacherously inflicted upon a citizen going abroad, exposing him as an alien and pointing him out for special reprobation and outrage.

Past, *n.* That part of Eternity with some small fraction of which we have a slight and regrettable acquaintance. A moving line called the Present parts it from an imaginary period known as the Future. These two grand divisions of Eternity, of which the one is continually effacing the other, are entirely unlike. The one is dark with sorrow and disappointment, the other, bright with prosperity and joy. The Past is the region of sobs, the Future is the realm of song. In one crouches Memory, clad in sackcloth and ashes, mumbling penitential prayer; in the sunshine of the other Hope flies with a free wing, beckoning to temples of success and bowers of ease. Yet the Past is the Future of yesterday, the Future is the Past of tomorrow. They are one – the knowledge and the dream.

Pastime, *n.* A device for promoting dejection. Gentle exercise for intellectual debility.

Patience, *n.* A minor form of despair, disguised as a virtue.

Patriot, *n.* One to whom the interests of a part seem superior to those of the whole. The dupe of statesmen and the tool of conquerors.

Patriotism, *n.* Combustible rubbish ready to the torch of any one ambitious to illuminate his name.

In Dr Johnson's famous dictionary patriotism is defined as the last resort of a scoundrel. With all due respect to an enlightened but inferior lexicographer I beg to submit that it is the first.

Peace, *n.* In international affairs, a period of cheating between two periods of fighting.

Pedestrian, *n.* The variable (and audible) part of the roadway for an automobile.

Pedigree, *n.* The known part of the route from an arboreal ancestor with a swim bladder to an urban descendant with a cigarette.

Penitent, *adj.* Undergoing or awaiting punishment.

Perfection, *n.* An imaginary state or quality distinguished from the actual by an element known as excellence; an attribute of the critic.

Peripatetic, *adj.* Walking about. Relating to the philosophy of Aristotle, who, while expounding it, moved from place to place in order to avoid his pupil's objections. A needless precaution – they knew no more of the matter than he.

Peroration, *n.* The explosion of an oratorical rocket. It dazzles, but to an observer having the wrong kind of nose its most conspicuous peculiarity is the smell of the several kinds of powder used in preparing it.

Perseverance, *n.* A lowly virtue whereby mediocrity achieves an inglorious success.

Pessimism, *n.* A philosophy forced upon the convictions of the observer by the disheartening prevalence of the optimist with his scarecrow hope and his unsightly smile.

Philanthropist, *n.* A rich (and usually bald) old gentleman who has trained himself to grin while his conscience is picking his pocket.

Philistine, *n.* One whose mind is the creature of its environment, following the fashion in thought, feeling and sentiment. He is sometimes learned, frequently prosperous, commonly clean and always solemn.

Philosophy, *n.* A route of many roads leading from nowhere to nothing.

Phonograph, *n.* An irritating toy that restores life to dead noises.

Photograph, *n.* A picture painted by the sun without instruction in art.

Physician, *n.* One upon whom we set our hopes when ill and our dogs when well.

Physiognomy, *n.* The art of determining the character of another by the resemblances and differences between his face and our own, which is the standard of excellence.

Piano, *n.* A parlor utensil for subduing the impenitent visitor. It is operated by depressing the keys of the machine and the spirits of the audience.

Picture, *n.* A representation in two dimensions of something wearisome in three.

Piety, *n.* Reverence for the Supreme Being, based upon His supposed resemblance to man.

Pig, *n.* An animal (*Porcus omnivorus*) closely allied to the human race by the splendor and vivacity of its appetite, which, however, is inferior in scope, for it sticks at pig.

Pilgrim, *n.* A traveler that is taken seriously. A Pilgrim Father was one who, leaving Europe in 1620 because not permitted to sing psalms through his nose, followed it to Massachusetts, where he could personate God according to the dictates of his conscience.

Pillory, *n.* A mechanical device for inflicting personal distinction – prototype of the modern newspaper conducted by persons of austere virtues and blameless lives.

Piracy, *n.* Commerce without its folly-swaddles, just as God made it.

PIANO

PANTALOONS

Pitiful, *adj.* The state of an enemy or opponent after an imaginary encounter with oneself.

Pity, *n.* A failing sense of exemption, inspired by contrast.

Plagiarism, *n.* A literary coincidence compounded of a discreditable priority and an honorable subsequence.

Plagiarize, *v.* To take the thought or style of another writer whom one has never, never read.

Plan, *v.t.* To bother about the best method of accomplishing an accidental result.

Platitude, *n.* The fundamental element and special glory of popular literature. A thought that snores in words that smoke. The wisdom of a million fools in the diction of a dullard. A fossil sentiment in artificial rock. A moral without the fable. All that is mortal of a departed truth. A demi-tasse of milk-and-morality. The Pope's-nose of a featherless peacock. A jelly-fish withering on the shore of the sea of thought. The cackle surviving the egg. A desiccated epigram.

Platonic, *adj.* Pertaining to the philosophy of Socrates. Platonic Love is a fool's name for the affection between a disability and a frost.

Plaudits, *n.* Coins with which the populace pays those who tickle and devour it.

Please, *v.* To lay the foundation for a superstructure of imposition.

Pleasure, *n.* The least hateful form of dejection.

Plebeian, *n.* An ancient Roman who in the blood of his country stained nothing but his hands. Distinguished from the Patrician, who was a saturated solution.

Plebiscite, *n.* A popular vote to ascertain the will of the sovereign.

Plenipotentiary, *adj.* Having full power. A Minister Plenipotentiary is a diplomatist possessing absolute authority on condition that he never exert it.

Pleonasm, *n.* An army of words escorting a corporal of thought.

Plow, *n.* An implement that cries aloud for hands accustomed to the pen.

Plunder, *v.* To take the property of another without observing the decent and customary reticences of theft. To effect a change of ownership with the candid concomitance of a brass band. To wrest the wealth of A from B and leave C lamenting a vanished opportunity.

Pocket, *n.* The cradle of motive and the grave of conscience. In woman this organ is lacking; so she acts without motive, and her conscience, denied burial, remains ever alive, confessing the sins of others.

Poetry, *n.* A form of expression peculiar to the Land beyond the Magazines.

Poker, *n.* A game said to be played with cards for some purpose to this lexicographer unknown.

Police, *n.* An armed force for protection and participation.

Politeness, *n.* The most acceptable hypocrisy.

Politics, *n.* A strife of interests masquerading as a contest of principles. The conduct of public affairs for private advantage.

Politician, *n.* An eel in the fundamental mud upon which the super-structure of organized society is reared. When he wriggles he mistakes the agitation of his tail for the trembling of the edifice. As compared with the statesman, he suffers the disadvantage of being alive.

Polygamy, *n.* A house of atonement, or expiatory chapel, fitted with several stools of repentance, as distinguished from monogamy, which has but one.

Portable, *adj.* Exposed to a mutable ownership through vicissitudes of possession.

Positive, *adj.* Mistaken at the top of one's voice.

Posterity, *n.* An appellate court which reverses the judgment of a popular author's contemporaries, the appellant being his obscure competitor.

Potable, *n.* Suitable for drinking. Water is said to be potable; indeed, some declare it our natural beverage, although even they find it palatable only when suffering from the recurrent disorder known as thirst, for which it is a medicine. Upon nothing has so great and diligent ingenuity been brought to bear in all ages and in all countries, except the most uncivilized, as upon the invention of substitutes for water. To hold that this general aversion to that liquid has no basis in the preservative instinct of the race is to be unscientific – and without science we are as the snakes and toads.

Poverty, *n.* A file provided for the teeth of the rats of reform. The number of plans for its abolition equals that of the reformers who suffer from it, plus that of the philosophers who know nothing about it. Its victims are distinguished by possession of all the virtues and by their faith in leaders seeking to conduct them into a prosperity where they believe these to be unknown.

Pray, *v.* To ask that the laws of the universe be annulled in behalf of a single petitioner confessedly unworthy.

Precedent, *n.* In Law, a previous decision, rule or practice which, in the absence of a definite statute, has whatever force and authority a Judge may choose to give it, thereby greatly simplifying his task of doing as he pleases. As there are precedents for everything, he has only to ignore those that make against his interest and accentuate those in the line of his desire. Invention of the precedent elevates the trial-at-law from the low estate of a fortuitous ordeal to the noble attitude of a dirigible arbitrament.

Precipitate, *adj.* Anteprandial.

Predestination, *n.* The doctrine that all things occur according to programme. This doctrine should not be confused with that of foreordination, which means that all things are programmed, but does not affirm their occurrence, that being only an implication from other doctrines by which this is entailed. The difference is great enough to have deluged Christendom with ink, to say nothing of the gore. With the distinction of the two doctrines kept well in mind, and a reverent belief in both, one may hope to escape perdition if spared.

Predicament, *n.* The wage of consistency.

Predilection, *n.* The preparatory stage of disillusion.

Preference, *n.* A sentiment, or frame of mind, induced by the erroneous belief that one thing is better than another.

An ancient philosopher, expounding his conviction that life is no better than death, was asked by a disciple why, then, he did not die.

'Because,' he replied, 'death is no better than life.'

It is longer.

Prehistoric, *adj.* Belonging to an early period and a museum. Antedating the art and practice of perpetuating falsehood.

Prejudice, *n.* A vagrant opinion without visible means of support.

Prelate, *n.* A church officer having a superior degree of holiness and a fat preferment. One of Heaven's aristocracy. A gentleman of God.

Prerogative, *n.* A sovereign's right to do wrong.

Presbyterian, *n.* One who holds the conviction that the governing authorities of the Church should be called presbyters.

Prescription, *n.* A physician's guess at what will best prolong the situation with least harm to the patient.

Present, *n.* That part of eternity dividing the domain of disappointment from the realm of hope.

Presentable, *adj.* Hideously appareled after the manner of the time and place.

Preside, *v.* To guide the action of a deliberative body to a desirable result.

Presidency, *n.* The greased pig in the field game of American politics.

President, *n.* The leading figure in a small group of men of whom – and of whom only it is positively known that immense numbers of their countrymen did not want any of them for President.

Prevaricator, *n.* A liar in the caterpillar state.

Price, *n.* Value, plus a reasonable sum for the wear and tear of conscience in demanding it.

Primate, *n.* The head of a church, especially a State church supported by involuntary contributions. The Primate of England is the Archbishop of Canterbury, an amiable old gentleman, who occupies Lambeth Palace when living and Westminster Abbey when dead. He is commonly dead.

Prison, *n.* A place of punishments and rewards. The poet assures us that

'Stone walls do not a prison make,'

but a combination of the stone wall, the political parasite and the moral instructor is no garden of sweets.

Private, *n.* A military gentleman with a field-marshal's baton in his knapsack and an impediment in his hope.

Proboscis, *n.* The rudimentary organ of an elephant which serves him in place of the knife-and-fork that Evolution has as yet denied him. For purposes of humor it is popularly called a trunk.

Projectile, *n.* The final arbiter in international disputes. Formerly these disputes were settled by physical contact of the disputants, with such simple arguments as the rudimentary logic of the times could supply the sword, the spear, and so forth. With the growth of prudence in military affairs the projectile came more and more into favor, and is now held in high esteem by the most courageous. Its capital defect is that it requires personal attendance at the point of propulsion.

Proof, *n.* Evidence having a shade more of plausibility than of unlikelihood. The testimony of two credible witnesses as opposed to that of only one.

Proof-reader, *n.* A malefactor who atones for making

your writing nonsense by permitting the compositor to make it unintelligible.

Property, *n.* Any material thing, having no particular value, that may be held by A against the cupidity of B. Whatever gratifies the passion for possession in one and disappoints it in all the others. The object of man's brief rapacity and long indifference.

Prophecy, *n.* The art and practice of selling one's credibility for future delivery.

Prospect, *n.* An outlook, usually forbidding. An expectation, usually forbidden.

Providential, *adj.* Unexpectedly and conspicuously beneficial to the person so describing it.

Prude, *n.* A bawd hiding behind the back of her demeanor.

Publish, *v.* In literary affairs, to become the fundamental element in a cone of critics.

Push, *n.* One of the two things mainly conducive to success, especially in politics. The other is Pull.

Queen, *n.* A woman by whom the realm is ruled when there is a king, and through whom it is ruled when there is not.

Quill, *n.* An implement of torture yielded by a goose and commonly wielded by an ass. This use of the quill is now obsolete, but its modern equivalent, the steel pen, is wielded by the same everlasting Presence.

Quiver, *n.* A portable sheath in which the ancient statesman and the aboriginal lawyer carried their lighter arguments.

Quixotic, *adj.* Absurdly chivalric, like Don Quixote. An insight into the beauty and excellence of this incomparable adjective is unhappily denied to him who has the misfortune to know that the gentleman's name is pronounced Ke-ho-tay.

Quorum, *n.* A sufficient number of members of a deliberative body to have their own way and their own way of having it. In the United States Senate a quorum consists of the chairman of the Committee on Finance and a messenger from the White House; in the House of Representatives, of the Speaker and the Devil.

Quotation, *n.* The act of repeating erroneously the words of another. The words erroneously repeated.

Quotient, *n.* A number showing how many times a sum of money belonging to one person is contained in the pocket of another – usually about as many times as it can be got there.

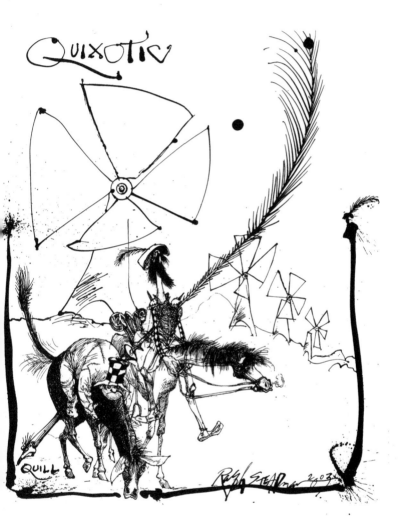

Rabble, *n.* In a republic, those who exercise a supreme authority tempered by fraudulent elections. The rabble is like the sacred Simurgh, of Arabian fable – omnipotent on condition that it do nothing.

Rack, *n.* An argumentative implement formerly much used in persuading devotees of a false faith to embrace the living truth. As a call to the unconverted the rack never had any particular efficacy, and is now held in light popular esteem.

Radicalism, *n.* The conservatism of tomorrow injected into the affairs of today.

Railroad, *n.* The chief of many mechanical devices

enabling us to get away from where we are to where we are no better off. For this purpose the railroad is held in highest favor by the optimist, for it permits him to make the transit with great expedition.

Ramshackle, *adj.* Pertaining to a certain order of architecture, otherwise known as the Normal American. Most of the public buildings of the United States are of the Ramshackle order, though some of our earlier architects preferred the Ironic. Recent additions to the White House in Washington are Theo-Doric, the ecclesiastic order of the Dorians. They are exceedingly fine and cost one hundred dollars a brick.

Rank, *n.* Relative elevation in the scale of human worth.

Ransom, *n.* The purchase of that which neither belongs to the seller, nor can belong to the buyer. The most unprofitable of investments.

Rapacity, *n.* Providence without industry. The thrift of power.

Rarebit, *n.* A Welsh rabbit, in the speech of the humorless, who point out that it is not a rabbit. To whom it may be solemnly explained that the comestible known as toad-in-the-hole is really not a toad, and that *riz-de-veau à la financière* is not the smile of a calf prepared after the recipe of a she banker.

Rascal, *n.* A fool considered under another aspect.

Rascality, *n.* Stupidity militant. The activity of a clouded intellect.

Rash, *adj.* Insensible to the value of our advice.

Rational, *adj.* Devoid of all delusions save those of observation, experience and reflection.

Reach, *n.* The radius of action of the human hand. The area within which it is possible (and customary) to gratify directly the propensity to provide.

Reading, *n.* The general body of what one reads. In our country it consists, as a rule, of Indiana novels, short stories in 'dialect' and humor in slang.

Realism, *n.* The art of depicting nature as it is seen by toads. The charm suffusing a landscape painted by a mole, or a story written by a measuring-worm.

Reality, *n.* The dream of a mad philosopher. That which would remain in the cupel if one should assay a phantom. The nucleus of a vacuum.

Really, *adv.* Apparently.

Rear, *n.* In American military matters, that exposed part of the army that is nearest to Congress.

Reason, *v.i.* To weigh probabilities in the scales of desire.

Reason, *n.* Propensitate of prejudice.

Reasonable, *adj.* Accessible to the infection of our own opinions. Hospitable to persuasion, dissuasion and evasion.

Rebel, *n.* A proponent of a new misrule who has failed to establish it.

Recollect, *v.* To recall with additions something not previously known.

Reconciliation, *n.* A suspension of hostilities. An armed truce for the purpose of digging up the dead.

Reconsider, *v.* To seek a justification for a decision already made.

Recount, *n.* In American politics, another throw of the dice, accorded to the player against whom they are loaded.

Recreation, *n.* A particular kind of dejection to relieve a general fatigue.

Recruit, *n.* A person distinguishable from a civilian by his uniform and from a soldier by his gait.

Redemption, *n.* Deliverance of sinners from the penalty of their sin, through their murder of the deity against whom they sinned. The doctrine of Redemption is the fundamental mystery of our holy religion, and whoso believeth in it shall not perish, but have everlasting life in which to try to understand it.

Redress, *n.* Reparation without satisfaction.

Red-skin, *n.* A North American Indian, whose skin is not red – at least not on the outside.

Referendum, *n.* A law for submission of proposed legislation to a popular vote to learn the nonsensus of public opinion.

Reflection, *n.* An action of the mind whereby we obtain a clearer view of our relation to the things of yesterday and are able to avoid the perils that we shall not again encounter.

Reform, *n.* A thing that mostly satisfies reformers opposed to reformation.

Regalia, *n.* Distinguishing insignia, jewels and costume of such ancient and honorable orders as Knights of Adam; Visionaries of Delectable Bosh; the Ancient Order of Modern Troglodytes; the League of Holy Humbug; the Golden Phalanx of Phalangers; the Genteel Society of Expurgated Hoodlums; the Mystic Alliance of Gorgeous Regalians; Knights and Ladies of the Yellow Dog; the Oriental Order of Sons of the West; the Blatherhood of Insufferable Stuff; Warriors of the Long Bow; Guardians of the Great Horn Spoon; the Band of Brutes; the Impenitent Order of Wife-Beaters; the Sublime Legion of Flamboyant Conspicuants; Worshipers at the Electroplated Shrine; Shining Inaccessibles; Fee-Faw-Fummers of the Inimitable Grip; Jannissaries of the Broad-Blown Peacock; Plumed Increscencies of the Magic Temple; the Grand Cabal of Able-Bodied Sedentarians; Associated Deities of the Butter Trade; the Garden of Galoots; the Affectionate Fraternity of Men Similarly Warted; the Flashing Astonishers; Ladies of Horror; Cooperative Association for Breaking into the Spotlight; Dukes of Eden; Disciples Militant of the Hidden Faith; Knights-Champions of the Domestic Dog; the Holy Gregarians; the Resolute Optimists; the Ancient Sodality of Inhospitable Hogs; Associated Sovereigns of Mendacity;

Dukes-Guardian of the Mystic Cesspool; the Society for Prevention of Prevalence; Kings of Drink; Polite Federation of Gents-Consequential; the Mysterious Order of the Undecipherable Scroll; Uniformed Rank of Lousy Cats; Monarchs of Worth and Hunger; Sons of the South Star; Prelates of the Tub-and-Sword.

Religion, *n.* A daughter of Hope and Fear, explaining to Ignorance the nature of the Unknowable.

Reliquary, *n.* A receptacle for such sacred objects as pieces of the true cross, short-ribs of saints, the ears of Balaam's ass, the lung of the cock that called Peter to repentance, and so forth. Reliquaries are commonly of metal, and provided with a lock to prevent the contents from coming out and performing miracles at unseasonable times.

Renown, *n.* A degree of distinction between notoriety and fame – a little more supportable than the one and a little more intolerable than the other. Sometimes it is conferred by an unfriendly and inconsiderate hand.

Reparation, *n.* Satisfaction that is made for a wrong and deducted from the satisfaction felt in committing it.

Repartee, *n.* Prudent insult in retort. Practiced by gentlemen with a constitutional aversion to violence, but a strong disposition to offend.

Repentance, *n.* The faithful attendant and follower of Punishment. It is usually manifest in a degree of reformation that is not inconsistent with continuity of sin.

RELIGION

REVOLUTION

Rational

REACH

REDEMPTION

Replica, *n.* A reproduction of a work of art, by the artist that made the original. It is so called to distinguish it from a 'copy,' which is made by another artist. When the two are made with equal skill the replica is the more valuable, for it is supposed to be more beautiful than it looks.

Reporter, *n.* A writer who guesses his way to the truth and dispels it with a tempest of words.

Repose, *v.i.* To cease from troubling.

Representative, *n.* In national politics, a member of the Lower House in this world, and without discernible hope of promotion in the next.

Republic, *n.* A nation in which, the thing governing and the thing governed being the same, there is only a permitted authority to enforce an optional obedience. In a republic the foundation of public order is the ever lessening habit of submission inherited from ancestors who, being truly governed, submitted because they had to. There are as many kinds of republics as there are gradations between the despotism whence they came and the anarchy whither they lead.

Requiem, *n.* A mass for the dead which the minor poets assure us the winds sing o'er the graves of their favorites. Sometimes, by way of providing a varied entertainment, they sing a dirge.

Resident, *adj.* Unable to leave.

Resign, *v.t.* To renounce an honor for an advantage. To renounce an advantage for a greater advantage.

Resolute, *adj.* Obstinate in a course that we approve.

Respectability, *n.* The offspring of a *liaison* between a bald head and a bank account.

Respirator, *n.* An apparatus fitted over the nose and mouth of an inhabitant of London, whereby to filter the visible universe in its passage to the lungs.

Respite, *n.* A suspension of hostilities against a sentenced assassin, to enable the Executive to determine whether the murder may not have been done by the prosecuting attorney. Any break in the continuity of a disagreeable expectation.

Responsibility, *n.* A detachable burden easily shifted to the shoulders of God, Fate, Fortune, Luck or one's neighbor. In the days of astrology it was customary to unload it upon a star.

Restitution, *n.* The founding or endowing of universities and public libraries by gift or bequest.

Retaliation, *n.* The natural rock upon which is reared the Temple of Law.

Retribution, *n.* A rain of fire-and-brimstone that falls alike upon the just and such of the unjust as have not procured shelter by evicting them.

Revelation, *n.* A famous book in which St John the

Divine concealed all that he knew. The revealing is done by the commentators, who know nothing.

Reverence, *n.* The spiritual attitude of a man to a god and a dog to a man.

Review, *v.t.*

> To set your wisdom (holding not a doubt of it,
> Although in truth there's neither bone nor skin to it)
> At work upon a book, and so read out of it
> The qualities that you have first read into it.

Revolution, *n.* In politics, an abrupt change in the form of misgovernment. Specifically, in American history, the substitution of the rule of an Administration for that of a Ministry, whereby the welfare and happiness of the people were advanced a full half-inch. Revolutions are usually accompanied by a considerable effusion of blood, but are accounted worth it − this appraisement being made by beneficiaries whose blood had not the mischance to be shed.

Ribaldry, *n.* Censorious language by another concerning oneself.

Rich, *adj.* Holding in trust and subject to an accounting the property of the indolent, the incompetent, the unthrifty, the envious, and the luckless. That is the view that prevails in the underworld, where the Brotherhood of Man finds its most logical development and candid advocacy. To denizens of the midworld the word means good and wise.

Ridicule, *n.* Words designed to show that the person of whom they are uttered is devoid of the dignity of character distinguishing him who utters them.

Right, *n.* Legitimate authority to be, to do, or to have; as the right to be a king, the right to do one's neighbor, the right to have measles, and the like.

Rime, *n.* Agreeing sounds in the terminals of verse, mostly bad. The verses themselves, as distinguished from prose, mostly dull. Usually (and wickedly) spelled 'rhyme.'

Rimer, *n.* A poet regarded with indifference or disesteem.

Riot, *n.* A popular entertainment given to the military by innocent bystanders.

R.I.P. A careless abbreviation of *requiescat in pace*, attesting an indolent goodwill to the dead.

Rite, *n.* A religious or semi-religious ceremony fixed by law, precept or custom, with the essential oil of sincerity carefully squeezed out of it.

Road, *n.* A strip of land along which one may pass from where it is too tiresome to be to where it is futile to go.

Robber, *n.* A candid man of affairs.

Romance, *n.* Fiction that owes no allegiance to the God of Things as They Are. In the novel the writer's thought is tethered to probability, as a domestic horse to the hitching-post, but in romance it ranges at will over the entire region of the imagination – free, lawless, immune to bit and rein. Your novelist is a poor creature, as Carlyle might say – a mere reporter. He may invent his characters and plot, but he must not imagine anything taking place that might not occur, albeit his entire narrative is candidly a lie. Why he imposes this hard condition on himself, and 'drags at each remove a lengthening chain' of his own forging he can explain in ten thick volumes without illuminating by so much as a candle's ray the black profound of his own ignorance of the matter. There are great novels, for great writers have 'laid waste their powers' to write them, but it remains true that far and away the most fascinating fiction that we have is 'The Thousand and One Nights.'

Rope, *n.* An obsolescent appliance for reminding assassins that they too are mortal.

Rostrum, *n.* In Latin, the beak of a bird or the prow of a ship. In American, a place from which a candidate for office energetically expounds the wisdom, virtue and power of the rabble.

Roundhead, *n.* A member of the Parliamentary party in the English civil war – so called from his habit of wearing his hair short, whereas his enemy, the Cavalier, wore his long. There were other points of difference between them, but the fashion in hair was the fundamental cause of quarrel. The Cavaliers were royalists because the king, an indolent fellow, found it more convenient to let his hair grow than to wash his neck. This the Roundheads, who were mostly barbers and soap-boilers, deemed an injury to trade, and the royal neck was therefore the object of their particular indignation. Descendants of the belligerents now wear their hair all alike, but the fires of animosity enkindled in that ancient strife smoulder to this day beneath the snows of British civility.

Rubbish, *n.* Worthless matter, such as the religions, philosophies, literatures, arts and sciences of the tribes infesting the regions lying due south from Boreaplas.

Rum, *n.* Generically, fiery liquors that produce madness in total abstainers.

Rumor, *n.* A favorite weapon of the assassins of character.

Russian, *n.* A person with a Caucasian body and a Mongolian soul. A Tartar Emetic.

Sabbath, *n.* A weekly festival having its origin in the fact that God made the world in six days and was arrested on the seventh. Among the Jews observance of the day was enforced by a Commandment of which this is the Christian version: 'Remember the seventh day to make thy neighbor keep it wholly.' To the Creator it seemed fit and expedient that the Sabbath should be the last day of the week, but the Early Fathers of the Church held other views.

Sacrament, *n.* A solemn religious ceremony to which several degrees of authority and significance are attached. Rome has seven sacraments, but the Protestant churches, being less prosperous, feel that they can afford only two, and these of inferior sanctity. Some of the smaller sects have no sacraments at all – for which mean economy they will indubitably be damned.

Sacred, *adj.* Dedicated to some religious purpose; having a divine character; inspiring solemn thoughts or emotions; as, the Dalai Lama of Thibet; the Moogum of M'bwango; the temple of Apes in Ceylon; the Cow in India; the Crocodile, the Cat and the Onion of ancient Egypt; the Mufti of Moosh; the hair of the dog that bit Noah, etc.

Saint, *n.* A dead sinner revised and edited.

Salamander, *n.* Originally a reptile inhabiting fire; later, an anthropomorphous immortal, but still a pyrophile. Salamanders are now believed to be extinct, the last one of which we have an account having been seen in Carcassonne by the Abbé Belloc, who exorcised it with a bucket of holy water.

Satan, *n.* One of the Creator's lamentable mistakes, repented in sash-cloth and axes. Being instated as an archangel, Satan made himself multifariously objection- able and was finally expelled from Heaven. Halfway in his descent he paused, bent his head in thought a moment and at last went back. 'There is one favor that I should like to ask,' said he.

'Name it.'

'Man, I understand, is about to be created. He will need laws.'

'What, wretch! you his appointed adversary, charged from the dawn of eternity with hatred of his soul – you ask for the right to make his laws?'

'Pardon; what I have to ask is that he be permitted to make them himself.'

It was so ordered.

Satiety, *n.* The feeling that one has for the plate after he has eaten its contents, madam.

Satire, *n.* An obsolete kind of literary composition in which the vices and follies of the author's enemies were expounded with imperfect tenderness. In this country satire never had more than a sickly and uncertain existence, for the soul of it is wit, wherein we are dolefully deficient, the humor that we mistake for it, like all humor, being tolerant and sympathetic. Moreover, although Americans are 'endowed by their Creator' with abundant vice and folly, it is not generally known that these are reprehensible qualities, wherefore the satirist is popularly regarded as a sour-spirited knave, and his every victim's outcry for codefendants evokes a national assent.

Sauce, *n.* The one infallible sign of civilization and enlightenment. A people with no sauces has one thousand vices; a people with one sauce has only nine hundred and ninety-nine. For every sauce invented and accepted a vice is renounced and forgiven.

Saw, *n.* A trite popular saying, or proverb. (Figurative and colloquial.) So called because it makes its way into a wooden head. Following are examples of old saws fitted with new teeth.

A penny saved is a penny to squander.

A man is known by the company that he organizes.

A bad workman quarrels with the man who calls him that.

A bird in the hand is worth what it will bring.

Better late than before anybody has invited you.

Example is better than following it.

Half a loaf is better than a whole one if there is much else.

Think twice before you speak to a friend in need.

What is worth doing is worth the trouble of asking somebody to do it.

Least said is soonest disavowed.

He laughs best who laughs least.

Speak of the Devil and he will hear about it.

Of two evils choose to be the least.

Strike while your employer has a big contract.

Where there's a will there's a won't.

Scarification, *n.* A form of penance practiced by the mediæval pious. The rite was performed, sometimes with a knife, sometimes with a hot iron, but always, says Arsenius Asceticus, acceptably if the penitent spared himself no pain nor harmless disfigurement. Scarification, with other crude penances, has now been superseded by benefaction.

The founding of a library or endowment of a university is said to yield to the penitent a sharper and more lasting pain than is conferred by the knife or iron, and is therefore a surer means of grace. There are, however, two grave objections to it as a penitential method: the good that it does and the taint of justice.

Scepter, *n.* A king's staff of office, the sign and symbol of his authority. It was originally a mace with which the sovereign admonished his jester and vetoed ministerial measures by breaking the bones of their proponents.

Scribbler, *n.* A professional writer whose views are antagonistic to one's own.

Scriptures, *n.* The sacred books of our holy religion, as distinguished from the false and profane writings on which all other faiths are based.

Seal, *n.* A mark impressed upon certain kinds of documents to attest their authenticity and authority. Sometimes it is stamped upon wax, and attached to the paper, sometimes into the paper itself. Sealing, in this sense, is a survival of an ancient custom of inscribing important papers with cabalistic words or signs to give them a magical efficacy independent of the authority that they represent. In the British Museum are preserved many ancient papers, mostly of a sacerdotal character, validated by necromantic pentagrams and other devices, frequently initial letters of words to conjure with; and in many instances these are attached in the same way that seals are appended now. As nearly every reasonless and apparently meaningless custom, rite or observance of modern times had origin in some remote utility, it is pleasing to note an example of ancient nonsense evolving in the process of ages into something really useful. Our word 'sincere' is derived from *sine cero*, without wax, but the learned are not in agreement as to whether this refers to the absence of the cabalistic signs, or to that of the wax with which letters were formerly closed from public scrutiny. Either view of the matter will serve one in immediate need of an hypothesis.

Seine, *n.* A kind of net for effecting an involuntary change of environment. For fish it is made strong and coarse, but women are more easily taken with a singularly delicate fabric weighted with small, cut stones.

Self-esteem, *n.* An erroneous appraisement.

Self-evident, *adj.* Evident to one's self and to nobody else.

Selfish, *adj.* Devoid of consideration for the selfishness of others.

Serial, *n.* A literary work, usually a story that is not true, creeping through several issues of a newspaper or magazine. Frequently appended to each instalment is a 'synopsis of preceding chapters' for those who have not read them, but a direr need is a synopsis of succeeding chapters for those who do not intend to read *them.* A synopsis of the entire work would be still better.

Sheriff, *n.* In America the chief executive officer of a county, whose most characteristic duties, in some of the

Western and Southern States, are the catching and hanging of rogues.

Siren, *n.* One of several musical prodigies famous for a vain attempt to dissuade Odysseus from a life on the ocean wave. Figuratively, any lady of splendid promise, dissembled purpose and disappointing performance.

Sophistry, *n.* The controversial method of an opponent, distinguished from one's own by superior insincerity and fooling.

Sorcery, *n.* The ancient prototype and forerunner of political influence.

Soul, *n.* A spiritual entity concerning which there hath been brave disputation. Plato held that those souls which in a previous state of existence (antedating Athens) had obtained the clearest glimpses of eternal truth entered into the bodies of persons who became philosophers. Plato was himself a philosopher. The souls that had least contemplated divine truth animated the bodies of usurpers and despots. Dionysius I, who had threatened to decapitate the broadbrowed philosopher, was a usurper and despot. Plato, doubtless, was not the first to construct a system of philosophy that could be quoted against his enemies; certainly he was not the last.

Story, *n.* A narrative, commonly untrue.

Success, *n.* The one unpardonable sin against one's fellows.

Suffrage, *n.* Expression of opinion by means of a ballot. The right of suffrage (which is held to be both a privilege and a duty) means, as commonly interpreted, the right to vote for the man of another man's choice, and is highly prized.

Sycophant, *n.* One who approaches Greatness on his belly so that he may not be commanded to turn and be kicked. He is sometimes an editor.

Syllogism, *n.* A logical formula consisting of a major and a minor assumption and an inconsequent. (*See* LOGIC.)

Sylph, *n.* An immaterial but visible being that inhabited the air when the air was an element and before it was fatally polluted by factory smoke, sewer gas and similar products of civilization. Sylphs were allied to gnomes, nymphs and salamanders, which dwelt, respectively, in earth, water and fire, all now insalubrious. Sylphs, like fowls of the air, were male and female, to no purpose, apparently, for if they had progeny they must have nested in inaccessible places, none of the chicks having ever been seen.

Symbol, *n.* Something that is supposed to typify or stand for something else. Many symbols are mere 'survivals' – things which having no longer any utility continue to exist because we have inherited the tendency to make them; as funereal urns carved on memorial monuments. They were once real urns holding the ashes of the dead. We cannot stop making them, but we can give them a name that conceals our helplessness.

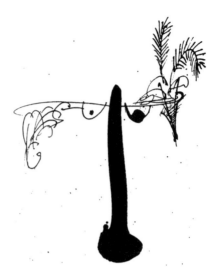

Table d' Hôte, *n.* A caterer's thrifty concession to the universal passion for irresponsibility.

Tail, *n.* The part of an animal's spine that has transcended its natural limitations to set up an independent existence in a world of its own.

Take, *v.t.* To acquire, frequently by force but preferably by stealth.

Talk, *v.t.* To commit an indiscretion without temptation, from an impulse without purpose.

Tariff, *n.* A scale of taxes on imports, designed to protect the domestic producer against the greed of his consumer.

Technicality, *n.* In an English court a man named Home was tried for slander in having accused a neighbor of murder. His exact words were: 'Sir Thomas Holt hath taken a cleaver and stricken his cook upon the head, so that one side of the head fell upon one shoulder and the other side upon the other shoulder.' The defendant was acquitted by instruction of the court, the learned judges holding that the words did not charge murder, for they did not affirm the death of the cook, that being only an inference.

Teetotaler, *n.* One who abstains from strong drink, sometimes totally, sometimes tolerably totally.

Telephone, *n.* An invention of the devil which abrogates some of the advantages of making a disagreeable person keep his distance.

Telescope, *n.* A device having a relation to the eye similar to that of the telephone to the ear, enabling distant objects to plague us with a multitude of needless details. Luckily it is unprovided with a bell summoning us to the sacrifice.

Tenacity, *n.* A certain quality of the human hand in its relation to the coin of the realm. It attains its highest development in the hand of authority and is considered a serviceable equipment for a career in politics.

Tomb, *n.* The House of Indifference. Tombs are now by common consent invested with a certain sanctity, but when they have been long tenanted it is considered no sin to break them open and rifle them, the famous Egyptologist, Dr Huggyns, explaining that a tomb may be innocently 'glened' as soon as its occupant is done 'smellynge,' the soul being then all exhaled. This reasonable view is now generally accepted by archæologists, whereby the noble science of Curiosity has been greatly dignified.

Tope, *v.* To tipple, booze, swill, soak, guzzle, lush, bib, or swig. In the individual, toping is regarded with disesteem, but toping nations are in the forefront of civilization and power. When pitted against the hard-drinking Christians the abstemious Mahometans go down like grass before the scythe. In India one hundred thousand beef-eating and brandy-and-soda guzzling Britons hold in subjection two hundred and fifty million vegetarian abstainers of the same Aryan race. With what an easy grace the whisky-loving American pushed the temperate Spaniard out of his possessions! From the time when the Berserkers ravaged all the coasts of Western Europe and lay drunk in every conquered port it has been the same way: everywhere the nations that drink too much are observed to fight rather well and not too righteously. Wherefore the estimable old ladies who abolished the canteen from the American army may justly boast of having materially augmented the nation's military power.

Tree, *n.* A tall vegetable intended by nature to serve as a penal apparatus, though through a miscarriage of justice most trees bear only a negligible fruit, or none at all. When naturally fruited, the tree is a beneficent agency of civilization and an important factor in public morals. In the stern West and the sensitive South its fruit (white and black respectively) though not eaten, is agreeable to the public taste and, though not exported, profitable to the general welfare.

Trial, *n.* A formal inquiry designed to prove and put upon record the blameless characters of judges, advocates and jurors. In order to effect this purpose it is necessary to supply a contrast in the person of one who is called the defendant, the prisoner, or the accused. If the contrast is made sufficiently clear this person is made to undergo such an affliction as will give the virtuous gentlemen a comfortable sense of their immunity, added to that of their worth.

Trinity, *n.* In the multiplex theism of certain Christian churches, three entirely distinct deities consistent with only one. Subordinate deities of the polytheistic faith, such as devils and angels, are not dowered with the power of combination, and must urge individually their claims to adoration and propitiation. The Trinity is one of the most sublime mysteries of our holy religion. In rejecting it because it is incomprehensible, Unitarians betray their inadequate sense of theological fundamentals. In religion we believe only what we do not understand, except in the instance of an intelligible doctrine that contradicts an incomprehensible one. In that case we believe the former as a part of the latter.

Truce, *n.* Friendship.

Truth, *n.* An ingenious compound of desirability and appearance. Discovery of truth is the sole purpose of philosophy, which is the most ancient occupation of the human mind and has a fair prospect of existing with increasing activity to the end of time.

Truthful, *adj.* Dumb and illiterate.

Trust, *n.* In American politics, a large corporation composed in greater part of thrifty working men, widows of small means, orphans in the care of guardians and the courts, with many similar malefactors and public enemies.

Turkey, *n.* A large bird whose flesh when eaten on certain religious anniversaries has the peculiar property of attesting piety and gratitude. Incidentally, it is pretty good eating.

Twice, *adv.* Once too often.

Type, *n.* Pestilent bits of metal suspected of destroying civilization and enlightenment, despite their obvious agency in this incomparable dictionary.

Tzetze (or Tsetse) Fly, *n.* An African insect (*Glossina morsitans*) whose bite is commonly regarded as nature's most efficacious remedy for insomnia, though some patients prefer that of the American novelist (*Mendax interminabilis*.)

Ubiquity, *n.* The gift or power of being in all places at one time, but not in all places at all times, which is omnipresence, an attribute of God and the luminiferous ether only. This important distinction between ubiquity and omnipresence was not clear to the mediæval Church and there was much bloodshed about it. Certain Lutherans, who affirmed the presence everywhere of Christ's body were known as Ubiquitarians. For this error they were doubtless damned, for Christ's body is present only in the eucharist, though that sacrament may be performed in more than one place simultaneously. In recent times ubiquity has not always been understood – not even by Sir Boyle Roche, for example, who held that a man cannot be in two places at once unless he is a bird.

Ugliness, *n.* A gift of the gods to certain women, entailing virtue without humility.

Ultimatum, *n.* In diplomacy, a last demand before resorting to concessions.

Un-American, *adj.* Wicked, intolerable, heathenish.

Unction, *n.* An oiling, or greasing. The rite of extreme unction consists in touching with oil consecrated by a bishop several parts of the body of one engaged in dying. Marbury relates that after the rite had been administered to a certain wicked English nobleman it was discovered that the oil had not been properly consecrated and no other could be obtained. When informed of this the sick man said in anger: 'Then I'll be damned if I die!'

'My son,' said the priest, 'that is what we fear.'

Understanding, *n.* A cerebral secretion that enables one having it to know a house from a horse by the roof on the house. Its nature and laws have been exhaustively expounded by Locke, who rode a house, and Kant, who lived in a horse.

Universalist, *n.* One who foregoes the advantage of a Hell for persons of another faith.

Urbanity, *n.* The kind of civility that urban observers ascribe to dwellers in all cities but New York. Its commonest expression is heard in the words, 'I beg your pardon,' and it is not inconsistent with disregard of the rights of others.

Uxoriousness, *n.* A perverted affection that has strayed to one's own wife.

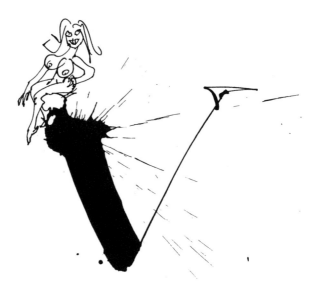

Valor, *n.* A soldierly compound of vanity, duty and the gambler's hope.

'Why have you halted?' roared the commander of a division at Chickamauga, who had ordered a charge; 'move forward, sir, at once.'

'General,' said the commander of the delinquent brigade, 'I am persuaded that any further display of valor by my troops will bring them into collision with the enemy.'

Vanity, *n.* The tribute of a fool to the worth of the nearest ass.

Virtues, *n. pl.* Certain abstentions.

Vituperation, *n.* Satire, as understood by dunces and all such as suffer from an impediment in their wit.

Vote, *n.* The instrument and symbol of a freeman's power to make a fool of himself and a wreck of his country.

Wall Street, *n.* A symbol of sin for every devil to rebuke. That Wall Street is a den of thieves is a belief that serves every unsuccessful thief in place of a hope in Heaven. Even the great and good Andrew Carnegie has made his profession of faith in the matter.

War, *n.* A by-product of the arts of peace. The most menacing political condition is a period of international amity. The student of history who has not been taught to expect the unexpected may justly boast himself inaccessible to the light. 'In time of peace prepare for war' has a deeper meaning than is commonly discerned; it means, not merely that all things earthly have an end – that change is the one immutable and eternal law – but that the soil of peace is thickly sown with seeds of war and singularly suited to their germination and growth. It was when Kubla Khan had decreed his 'stately pleasure dome' – when, that is to say, there were peace and fat feasting in Xanadu – that he

> heard from far
> Ancestral voices prophesying war.

One of the greatest of poets, Coleridge was one of the wisest of men, and it was not for nothing that he read us this parable. Let us have a little less of 'hands across the sea,' and a little more of that elemental distrust that is the security of nations. War loves to come like a thief in the night; professions of eternal amity provide the night.

Washingtonian, *n.* A Potomac tribesman who exchanged the privilege of governing himself for the advantage of good government. In justice to him it should be said that he did not want to.

Weaknesses, *n. pl.* Certain primal powers of Tyrant Woman wherewith she holds dominion over the male of her species, binding him to the service of her will and paralyzing his rebellious energies.

Weather, *n.* The climate of an hour. A permanent topic of conversation among persons whom it does not interest, but who have inherited the tendency to chatter about it from naked arboreal ancestors whom it keenly concerned. The setting up of official weather bureaus and their maintenance in mendacity prove that even

governments are accessible to suasion by the rude fore-fathers of the jungle.

Wedding, *n.* A ceremony at which two persons undertake to become one, one undertakes to become nothing, and nothing undertakes to become supportable.

Werewolf, *n.* A wolf that was once, or is sometimes, a man. All werewolves are of evil disposition, having assumed a bestial form to gratify a bestial appetite, but some, transformed by sorcery, are as humane as is consistent with an acquired taste for human flesh.

Whangdepootenawah, *n.* In the Ojibwa tongue, disaster; an unexpected affliction that strikes hard.

Wheat, *n.* A cereal from which a tolerably good whiskey can with some difficulty be made, and which is used also for bread. The French are said to eat more bread per capita of population than any other people, which is natural, for only they know how to make the stuff palatable.

White, *adj.* and *n.* Black.

Widow, *n.* A pathetic figure that the Christian world has agreed to take humorously, although Christ's tenderness towards widows was one of the most marked features of his character.

Wine, *n.* Fermented grape-juice known to the Women's Christian Union as 'liquor,' sometimes as 'rum.' Wine, madam, is God's next best gift to man.

Wit, *n.* The salt with which the American humorist spoils his intellectual cookery by leaving it out.

Witch, *n.* (1) An ugly and repulsive old woman, in a wicked league with the Devil. (2) A beautiful and attractive young woman, in wickedness a league beyond the Devil.

Witticism, *n.* A sharp and clever remark, usually quoted, and seldom noted; what the Philistine is pleased to call a 'joke.'

Woman, *n.* An animal usually living in the vicinity of Man, and having a rudimentary susceptibility to domestication. It is credited by many of the elder zoologists with a certain vestigial docility acquired in a former state of seclusion, but naturalists of the post-susananthony period, having no knowledge of the seclusion, deny the virtue and declare that such as creation's dawn beheld, it roareth now. The species is the most widely distributed of all beasts of prey, infesting all habitable parts of the globe, from Greenland's spicy mountains to India's moral strand. The popular name (wolf-man) is incorrect, for the creature is of the cat kind. The woman is lithe and graceful in its movements, especially the American variety (*Felis pugnans*), is omnivorous, and can be taught not to talk.

Worship, *n.* A popular form of abjection, having an element of pride.

Wrath, *n.* Anger of a superior quality and degree, appropriate to exalted characters and momentous occasions; as, 'the wrath of God,' 'the day of wrath,' etc.

X in our alphabet being a needless letter has an added invincibility to the attacks of the spelling reformers, and like them, will doubtless last as long as the language. X is the sacred symbol of ten dollars, and in such words as Xmas, Xn, etc., stands for Christ, not, as is popularly supposed, because it represents a cross, but because the corresponding letter in the Greek alphabet is the initial of His name – Χριστός. If it represented a cross it would stand for St Andrew, who 'testified' upon one of that shape. In the algebra of psychology *x* stands for Woman's mind. Words beginning with X are Grecian and will not be defined in this standard English dictionary.

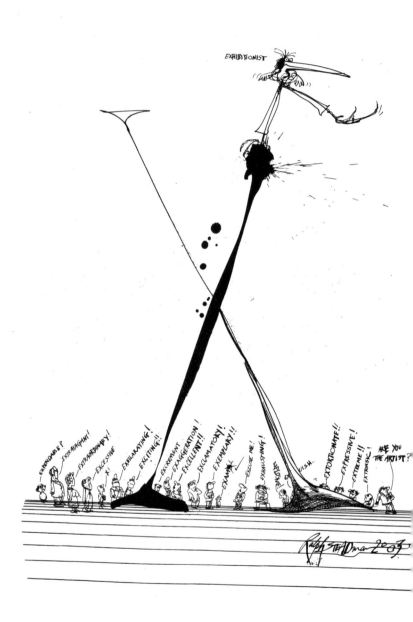

Yankee, *n.* In Europe, an American. In the Northern States of our Union, a New Englander. In the Southern States the word is unknown.

Year, *n.* A period of three hundred and sixty-five disappointments.

Yesterday, *n.* The infancy of youth, the youth of manhood, the entire past of age.

Yoke, *n.* An implement, madam, to whose Latin name, *jugum*, we owe one of the most illuminating words in our language – a word that defines the matrimonial situation with precision, point and poignancy. A thousand apologies for with-holding it.

Youth, *n.* The Period of Possibility, when Archimedes finds a fulcrum, Cassandra has a following and seven cities compete for the honor of endowing a living Homer.

Youth is the true Saturnian Reign, the Golden Age on earth again, when figs are grown on thistles, and pigs betailed with whistles and, wearing silken bristles, live ever in clover, and cows fly over, delivering milk at every door, and Justice never is heard to snore, and every assassin is made a ghost and, howling, is cast into Baltimost!

Zany, *n.* A popular character in old Italian plays, who imitated with ludicrous incompetence the *buffone*, or clown, and was therefore the ape of an ape; for the clown himself imitated the serious characters of the play. The zany was progenitor to the specialist in humor, as we today have the unhappiness to know him. In the zany we see an example of creation; in the humorist, of transmission. Another excellent specimen of the modern zany is the curate, who apes the rector, who apes the bishop, who apes the archbishop, who apes the devil.

Zeal, *n.* A certain nervous disorder afflicting the young and inexperienced. A passion that goeth before a sprawl.

Zeus, *n.* The chief of Grecian gods, adored by the Romans as Jupiter and by the modern Americans as God, Gold, Mob and Dog. Some explorers who have touched upon the shores of America, and one who professes to have penetrated a considerable distance into the interior, have thought that these four names stand for as many distinct deities, but in his monumental work on Surviving Faiths, Frumpp insists that the natives are monotheists, each having no other god than himself, whom he worships under many sacred names.

Zigzag, *v.t.* To move forward uncertainly, from side to side, as one carrying the white man's burden. (From *zed*, z, and *jag*, an Icelandic word of unknown meaning.)

Zoology, *n.* The science and history of the animal kingdom, including its king, the House Fly (*Musca maledicta*). The father of zoology was Aristotle, as is universally conceded, but the name of its mother has not come down to us. Two of the science's most illustrious expounders were Buffon and Oliver Goldsmith, from both of whom we learn (*L'Histoire générale des animaux* and *A History of Animated Nature*) that the domestic cow sheds its horns every two years.

ZOOLOGY

Ralph STEADman 2003

A NOTE ON THE AUTHOR

Ambrose Bierce was a veteran of the American Civil War who fought at Shiloh and Chickamauga in the Union ranks. After the war he became one of America's best-known writers and journalists. His collected works, including many spine-chilling gothic stories, were published in eight volumes in his lifetime, but he is best remembered for two books of stories – *Tales of Soldiers and Civilians* (1891) and *Can Such Things Be?* (1893) – and, of course, *The Devil's Dictionary* (1911). In 1913 he set off for Mexico, then in the throes of revolution, and was never seen again.

Angus Calder is the author of *The People's War* (1969), *Revolutionary Empire* (1981) and *Gods, Mongrels and Demons: 101 Brief but Essential Lives* (2003).

A NOTE ON THE ILLUSTRATOR

Ralph Steadman is the author/illustrator of many books including *Sigmund Freud, I Leonardo, The Big I Am and The Scar-Strangled Banner*. He is also the illustrator of *Alice* and *Animal Farm*, and of Hunter S. Thompson's infamous *Fear and Loathing in Las Vegas*. His most recent publication is the novel *Doodaaa*.

A NOTE ON THE TYPE

The text of this book is set in Bembo, the original types for which were cut by Francesco Griffo for the Venetian printer Aldus Manutius, and were first used in 1495 for Cardinal Bembo's *De Aetna*. Claude Garamond (1480–1561) used Bembo as a model, and so it became the front-runner of standard European type for the following two centuries. Its modern form was designed, following the original, for Monotype in 1929 and is widely in use today.

The display face is Cheltenham Spa bold, designed by Ralph Steadman in 1994 at the Cheltenham Festival of Literature, England.